I0568139

Paperback ISBN: 978-1-990843-03-7

Ebook ISBN:978-1-990843-04-4

Audiobook ISBN:978-1-990843-06-8

CONTENTS

CLUTTER-FREE YOUR HOME

Secrets To Declutter, Clean And Organise Your
Home. The Ultimate Guide With Ideas, Habits And
Plans For A Perfectly Organized Life

Noelle Gill

A dirty and messy house:

WHAT IS THE CONNECTION WITH OUR PSYCHOLOGY?

CHAPTER 1 YOUR MESSY HOUSE AFFECTS YOUR WELL-BEING

The world is beautiful because it is varied and this is also true of the care of domestic spaces. If on the one hand, in fact, there are those who organize their environment in a precise and orderly way, on the other hand there are those who tend to have a less "rigid" and methodical management, if not ... chaos! Given that confusion and dirt are two different things (even if sometimes disorder can lead to a dirtier house, because it makes it more difficult to clean thoroughly), what is the link between a house in disorder and our psychology? Let's see together.

A dirty and messy house: what is the connection with our psychology?

A house can be dirty and untidy for several reasons. In addition to the "psychology" that could be hidden behind certain ways of acting, the reason why a house is neglected is often linked to the hectic pace of today's life that absorbs time and energy. This does not mean that the house should be left to itself, of course, but it is not always easy, without a doubt, to keep everything clean and "spotless" as you would like. There are also people who, compared to perfectly organized environments as with a minimalist style, instead prefer spaces rich in objects and a less set order, or who tend to give less priority to household chores in general (in this case, of course, the important thing is never neglect the healthiness and liveability of the house, which remain fundamental aspects for the well-being of the person).

Of course, as we will see, there is a limit to everything and there are circumstances in which excessive disorder is no longer a simple way of being, but can represent the symptom of a deeper discomfort.

Disorder as a synonym for creativity

In the collective imagination, disorder is often associated with creativity and imagination, a connection that has also been confirmed by research conducted by the Carlson School of Management of the University of Minnesota, according to which a disorderly environment favors creativity. How did the study take place? The participants involved were distributed in two different rooms, one tidy and the other untidy: the people who were in the untidy room were shown to develop more innovative ideas (they were asked to propose new possible uses for ping pong balls) and also a greater propensity for novelty.

Good news also for lovers of order, however: according to this experiment, an orderly environment would stimulate healthy food choices and generous behaviors. To support the advantages of order, research was carried out by Princeton University which showed that disorder would make concentration more difficult. Additionally, a study published in the journal Personality and Social Psychology Bulletin found that women who described their home as untidy showed higher levels of the stress hormone cortisol.

Although there are different personalities who prefer more or less orderly environments, there is a limit beyond which disorder and neglect can be the indicator of a problem. The domestic environment, in fact, can represent a projection of the individual's state of mind and when chaos triumphs, becoming ungovernable, it could signal an inner discomfort (for example the inability to make decisions, to leave the past behind, etc.) and also hide serious psychological problems; in the same way, too maniacal and obsessive care of the house can also be a sign of malaise.

Given that extremes never go well, therefore, trying to keep clutter in the house under control is also very important for easy cleaning. As mentioned previously, in fact, although disorder and cleanliness are two different things, excessive confusion risks demotivation and making household chores more difficult and tiring. To better manage the home, despite the work and the many commitments, a solution - if you have the possibility - can be to rely on a domestic worker (even once every 1 or 2 weeks, for example, or on the occasion of more demanding cleaning).

The dreams we have, sometimes, can reveal the state of mind we are living in a given period of life. Dreaming of a house in disorder, for example, could suggest that we are going through a moment of confusion and emotional instability, sensations that would also manifest themselves through the images of a chaotic and upside-down environment.

An untidy house "confuses" the brain and sleep is also affected

Not only does living in chaos generate more anxiety, but it also induces you to eat more with consequences on weight. Recent research has shown that those who love to tidy up usually have better cardiovascular health.

It is a law of physics, the second law of thermodynamics: all natural processes involve an increase in entropy. That is, they lead to a system in which the degree of order of the elements decreases. Translated, it is in the nature of things to tend to disorder if we do not intervene with a little effort: if we do not wash the dishes, dirty dishes will accumulate in the sink; if we do not put the books back on the shelves, piles will form on the floor, and so on. Some more, some less, we all try to oppose the chaos and do well, since order is also helpful to staying healthy. Living in a house where there are too many things piled up, for example, can compromise sleep: Pamela Thacher, a psychologist at St. Lawrence University in the United States, has shown that disorder in a room reduces the quality of rest and this can then translate into stress, anxiety, increased appetite and everything else that can result from disturbed sleep, including poorer cognitive performance. Data also confirmed by a survey by the US National Sleep Foundation, according to which those who do not tolerate seeing the bed unmade and make it carefully every morning have a 19 percent more chance of sleeping well (and if the sheets are always clean, rest is even better for 75 percent of respondents).

Cluttered kitchen, goodbye diet

Some time ago then Lenny Vartanian of the University of New South Wales in Sidney, Australia, demonstrated on a group of volunteers that having the kitchen cluttered with dirty dishes, with pans and pots lying around and bulk food on the shelves leads to eating more and choosing less healthy foods, such as chocolate chip cookies instead of fruit. On the other hand, those who find themselves in a clean and tidy kitchen resist temptation, even if they are under stress: the combination of a chaotic environment and the feeling of anxiety is fatal, and in the long run can even lead to putting on a few extra pounds. If the house is in order, however, according to data collected by psychologists at the University of Los Angeles in California, anxiety and depression, are less likely; on the contrary, living in apartments full of stacked objects increases the production of cortisol, the stress hormone.

Exercise

Lovers of order are generally in better health than those who spend their days in rooms that have not seen a broom or vacuum cleaner for some time: a research by Purdue University in Indianapolis has shown this on a thousand people followed for over ten years, noting that order was directly related to the degree of physical activity and overall cardiovascular health. "The confusion present in the rooms of the house was found to be a parameter for predicting the state of health, better than the livability of the neighborhood," says the author, Nicole Keith. "Spending part of the day cleaning, using the washing machine, dusting, and the rest is to be considered real physical exercise, which helps to keep you active and healthy". The reasons why a clean house without too many objects around makes us feel good, however, do not pass only from the calories spent on household chores, but also from the innate preferences of the brain, which loves order and regularity to the point of looking for it even when it's not there: we tend to see regular patterns everywhere, even in the absence of a "thread" that binds objects, and we don't want too many things in the visual field, because they distract us and make us waste cognitive energy.

Cognitive performance

The demonstration comes from research by the Princeton Neuroscience Institute, which by analyzing the brain activity of those in more or less chaotic environments with magnetic resonance has verified how order is accompanied by a greater ability to focus on what matters and better information processing. Corollary: if there are no piles of useless documents, blunt pencils and the like on the desk, we work better and are more productive, we do not postpone the most important tasks and cognitive performance improves thanks to more focused attention on what is really needed, rather than to the crumpled pages beside the computer screen. Confusion alarms the brain, which in fact gives the signal to produce more cortisol, and the same happens if the chaos is in one's thoughts: Jacob Hirsh, of the Rotman School of Management at the University of Toronto, coined the term psychological entropy to indicate the "uncertain" thoughts that become gradually more confused and generate anxiety.

Excess of stimuli

Chaos in the mind is favored by the excess of stimuli we are subjected to today: according to Daniel Levitin, professor of psychology and behavioral neuroscience at McGill University in Montreal, "The load of information to which we are exposed in the last twenty-five years has quintupled and today in our free time alone we process about a hundred thousand words, the equivalent of 34 gigabytes. The brain, however, has a processing capacity of 120 bits per second, listening to another person "occupies" 60. It means that we cannot really be multitasking, but we must also put order in our heads by giving priority to what is needed gradually really pay attention". Making a list of tasks to take care of in order not to waste cognitive energy or setting smartphone notifications to remind us to switch to something else when it's time to do so are therefore good methods to "clear the brain" of the disorder of thoughts, helping it to concentrate on one thing at a time and thus to work better.

CHAPTER 2 THE BENEFITS OF HAVING AN ORGANIZED AND TIDY HOME

Tidying up and cleaning the house: therapy for the body and mind.

The home is one of the places where we spend a lot of time: taking care of your home is a bit like taking care of yourself.

There is a profound link between man and the environment where he lives, both at the macro level, that is, at the level of the place in a broad sense, and at the micro level, that is our home.

Living the space

From an anthropological point of view there is a profound correlation between space and body. In fact, as the anthropologist Vanessa Maher points out, already from the verb "cure" that is used in reference to "take care of the house", it refers to an act that normally refers to the body or the self (take care of oneself).

Anthropologist Mary Douglas also talks about how dirt is seen as a symptom of disorder in any society and must be combated as such. Dirt leads to confusion and contamination, and that is why it is necessary to have order.

The categories clean / dirty, order / disorder become a metaphor to categorize not only environments, but also people and their acceptance in society.

If from a social level the space we live in is a representation, in part, of what we are, how do we experience this space and its care on a psychological level?

Tidying up the house to order the mind

On a psychological level, tidying up the house is seen as a way of tidying up and clearing our minds too. In fact, the conditions of the environment in which we live can affect our mental state: for this reason putting things in order and arranging, can help us to arrange and put order among our thoughts. Similarly, procrastinating and leaving the house in disorder can be due to a moment of mental chaos and could steal energy from our daily life, preventing us from carrying out other activities.

Two things need to be pointed out:

- in some cases the disorder can be associated with creative people who find order in their disorder.
- manic house cleaning isn't good - it could be an indicator of deeper distress related to obsessive-compulsive disorder.

Cleanliness and order, like other daily activities and behavioral traits, are not absolute truths, but everyone must find comfort and balance within a spectrum of possibilities that make them feel good.

At the level of interpersonal relationships with the people we live with, it is important to create and maintain some healthy (and non-toxic) behaviors to better enjoy the environment in which we live: our home is our refuge.

Negative relationships and toxic behaviors in the home.

The home should generally be a comfortable place, where we feel loved and where well-being prevails. This does not only mean creating a physical space in which to feel good, but also trying to avoid having toxic behaviors towards the people who are living with us, whether they are family members, partners or roommates.

It is important to have respect for others and for the space in which we live, in order not to create a toxic and negative environment.

Let's delve into some negative behaviors that would be best left outside the front door.

Shouting: Shouting means wanting to impose one's will on others and can be a form of violence and an attempt to make the other submit. On children in particular, this behavior can cause damage to the level of personality and emotional balance, but even in the case of adults this attitude certainly does not create pleasant situations. Shouting is just a symptom of a lack of control and an inability to handle the situation.

Hostility: Negativity and hostility are feelings that are palpable in the air. And if this type of behavior persists among the inhabitants of a house, it could be very difficult and distressing to spend time in our home. Above all it could be very difficult to relax and rest in such an environment, thus worsening our general living conditions. We must try to solve problems and not generate conflicts, learning to communicate and get involved, respecting others and ourselves.

Drama: We all go through dramatic moments throughout our lives. But there are people who live as if every day were a drama, living everything with negativity and creating problems where they don't exist. If we are near one of these people (or if we are the person in question) we could find ourselves in an environment that gradually becomes toxic and pessimistic, infected by the negative attitude. What can we do in these cases? Again it is important to try to communicate with these people, showing them how the attitude they have is conditioning everyone and creating a negative environment. We could try to offer them positive alternatives and a more serene atmosphere for everyday life.

Confusion. We have seen how confusion and disorder in an environment can affect or be a reflection of an equally confused state of mind. In this sense it can generate stress and our brain at the same time has more difficulty in processing information. Confusion can lead to a feeling of saturation which affects our well-being and productivity. It is important to have rules at home, which clearly define the limits and roles of coexistence, to find yourself in a positive, orderly and clean environment.

Denigration. Above all within a family, if the people who are part of it are constantly denigrated by others, it may make some difficult moments, besides the fact of causing low self-esteem and difficulties later in life. There are different types of denigration: from judging someone by assigning them a role, for example that of black sheep, or by attributing to them skills or not. This negatively affects both the person in question but also all members of the family, because no one identifies well what is right or wrong, as well as responsibilities and consequences. If we find ourselves in such a situation, to try to get out of it we can first try to understand and make it clear that each person has an intrinsic value and that each has qualities and defects that are worth knowing and experiencing.

Furnish, clean and rearrange your space to take care of yourself.

We have already said how to clean, order and beautify your home, is good for the body, spirit and mind.

We think of spring cleaning, tidying up after the cold of winter, fresh air coming in through the windows and the renewal of the wardrobe.

But how can spring cleaning make us feel better?

According to experts, cleaning the house has several beneficial effects:

Cleaning the house kills germs and bacteria, leading to a clean house that strengthens your immune system and helps avoid disease.

In addition, a tidy and clean home helps reduce stress and accidents in the home, and prevents depression.

It promotes concentration and reflection in difficult or very intense periods.

Some studies link order and cleanliness with the decision to follow an active lifestyle and a healthier diet.

ARE YOU READY TO IMPROVE YOUR WELL-BEING?

There are many ancient and traditional views, both in our culture and in the oriental one, which study and deepen the concept of reorganization and architecture as a means to foment well-being.

Below we will focus on two visions: the philosophy of feng shui and the Konmari method (whose main exponent is Marie Kondo).

We have chosen these methods because we believe there are important points for reflection and suggestions, and not necessarily because they must be followed to the letter. Let's take a closer look at them!

Seeking well-being through Feng Shui

Feng shui is an ancient art that developed in China and that starts from the study of nature and its rules to apply them to homes and architecture. Feng Shui means respectively wind and water, and they are the two main elements on which settlement choices were made in the past: they are the elements that shape life with their actions.

To apply Feng Shui within your own space, you normally resort to an expert, but we can leave some tips here:

Symmetry: the floor plan of the house should be square or rectangular (i.e. as symmetrical as possible), to avoid dead spots (although this problem can be overcome by inserting tall furniture).

Cardinal points: the internal layout of the rooms must follow the cardinal points. The entrance is preferable to the north, while the rooms for relationships are located in the south.

Colors: the colors are related to the different rooms. Warm colors will be used in south facing rooms, while cool colors will be used in north facing rooms.

Furniture: furniture and furnishings must be arranged in such a way as not to obstruct the flow (and passage) that flows into a room. So it is best to avoid sharp and bulky furniture. As for the position of the bed in FengShui, it is normally recommended to place the head of the bed facing North, but in reality it depends on some variables related to the layout of the room (for example, more or less proximity to the door).

The 5 elements: Feng Shui also recommends to include in the furniture, decorations that allow you to control the 5 elements (for example an aquarium for water, iron objects (metal), plants (wood), vases (earth), candles (fire).

Large windows with a regular shape, which should however be placed not in front of the door.

Harmonious interior and exterior. If you have an outdoor space it is important to "cultivate" it so that it is in harmony with the internal space ... and the presence of plants and a vegetable garden helps the mind and body!

Eliminate the superfluous. According to Feng Shui, objects we don't use steal our energy and transmit negative energy to us. We must leave the energy to flow freely.

The Konmari and Marie Kondo method

Marie Kondo is the author of the book "The Magic Power of Tidying" which tries to find the best way to tidy up the house (and the mind).

Some of the basics are:

Boomerang effect: tidying up the house means not only tidying up, but also getting rid of the things we don't need. Because if we accumulate things, even if we try to put them in order, sooner or later we will end up with the house being full of things scattered throughout.

Learning to throw away what we don't need. This means letting go and giving things up. Among the objects there are some that have a meaning that is visceral and makes us happy, while others leave us indifferent. If in front of an object we find ourselves uncertain whether to throw it or not, then we probably don't really care but we are victims of a neurotic impulse. Indifferent objects obstruct the house, and therefore it is important to get rid of them. But first we have to find a moment, to thank the object and greet it (so as not to feel guilty feelings and give value to the object and the effort we made to buy it).

To accomplish this task, the Marie Kondo method is developed through 9 steps, to be carried out one after the other and passing to the next only when the first is completed.

Throw away everything that is indifferent to us and that has no meaning for us (always remembering to thank and say hello).

Keep only what brings happiness and well-being to our life.

One thing at a time: sort by categories, not by area. For example, start with the closet, not with the whole room! Start with clothes: it's an easier choice, because we know what we wear and what we don't.

Organize the clothes vertically, making small triangles and then hanging them, A sort of clothing library.

Don't put it off. It is important to start and finish each category.

Keep the objects of value. Everything around you must make sense.

Carry out this work yourself, because together with others you may get confused, postpone or make you decide not to throw out objects.

Don't spend money on furniture. Very often it will be enough to order in the right way and throw away the superfluous to make the available furniture suffice.

There are many benefits to living in an orderly house, one of these is to be able to create a relaxing and welcoming environment that stimulates you to seek even interior order. Think about it, whenever you need to concentrate in a completely natural and instinctive way, you prefer to choose an orderly environment.

This is because order favors reasoning and allows you to organize ideas more easily and without distractions. While clutter often causes confusion and conveys negative feelings.

WHY PUT THE HOUSE IN ORDER?

This is because by eliminating the superfluous, you begin to put in order a little bit inside yourself too.

Ordering stimulates you to change your attitude, transform your home and make it closer to what you want, it can be the starting point for a deeper and more radical change.

HOW TO SUCCEED IN ORDERING THE HOUSE

Now that you understand the reasons why you should tidy up the place where you live and the benefits it can offer you, it's time to get some practical advice.

I know how difficult it is to put the house in order, and to maintain over time the result you have achieved after so much effort, and that's why here you will find three simple steps that you can follow to put everything in its place.

Take care of your home and turn it into your refuge, a place to feel good. You will find that with the right strategies and a little good will it is not that difficult to succeed.

1. Eliminate the unnecessary

Look around and begin to notice how many superfluous things surround you, how many things you have kept over the years without any real use.

Separate them from everything else and decide whether to throw them away or donate them, but discard them. You will have more awareness of what you really need and avoid piling up unnecessary things in the future by creating more space for you and the things that really matter.

2. Organize the spaces

Organize your things so that they are functional and comfortable. Each person has a different method, look for the solution that best suits your space and your needs. It is often difficult to keep the house tidy simply because it is tiring and laziness sooner or later always takes over. It is therefore necessary to minimize the effort required. If storing your things in the space you have created for them costs you as much as leaving them scattered around the house, you will be more likely to put them away. Think about this and use boxes, dividers and binders to make tidying up your home as easy and quick as possible. Since you have to be realistic and we all know that a little clutter is inevitable, limit it only in certain areas. It will be easier this way, to keep it under control and prevent it from regaining the upper hand.

3. Don't accumulate

If you have succeeded in following steps 1 and 2 your home will now be tidy and well organized. You will have spent time and energy to fix everything, not to ruin the work done.

This hard-won order is often threatened by the inability to arrange your new purchases in the right spaces. Whenever you introduce something new into the house, store it following the organization you have adopted in a functional way, do not arrange it randomly as you would have done before. When you no longer need it, eliminate it, so as to avoid being overwhelmed again by useless things that if not managed correctly, will accumulate day after day making you return to the starting point. Get rid of superfluous things that sooner or later you will find yourself having to throw away. Make tidying up a daily habit.

If you follow all three steps you can finally feel free from clutter and enjoy your space. You've earned it, take advantage of it by filling it with what you love.

Starting to take care of the environment in which you live and spend your free time is the first step to take care of yourself.

CHAPTER 3 DISORDER TRIGGERS STRESS AND ANXIETY

Clutter in the house triggers stress and anxiety, says a psychologist.

Does it also happen to you when you return home, perhaps after a long and stressful day, to find every room completely in disorder? In a single instant, your desire to chase away the stress by closing the front door fails. At this point, usually, a nervousness emerges that lasts throughout the evening, along with stress and anxiety.

Don't worry, you are not the only one to have such a response to disorder, nor are you wrong to have it: according to psychologists. In fact, messy spaces are the trigger for stress and panic attacks.

"Clutter greatly affects how we feel in our homes, offices or elsewhere. Spaces crowded with cluttered things trigger a state of anxiety, make us feel helpless and overwhelmed. People rarely recognize that it's the clutter that is the cause of the stress in their lives," said psychologist Sherrie Bourg Carter.

Disorder, therefore, could play a much more influential role in our mental well-being than we have ever thought.

It causes mental fatigue because it exposes us to a large number of useless stimuli;

It takes our attention away from what we really want to focus on;

It tells the brain that our work is not done yet;

It leads us to think about the effort and time it will take to put everything in order.

In all this there is a solution, the simplicity of which depends both on one's willpower and on the presence or absence of other people who can contribute to the disorder.

According to the psychologist, in the event that the house is inhabited by a family, it is good to involve all the family members in the tidying process. You can think of assigning a room each or of establishing one day a week dedicated to cleaning the rooms.

One way to prevent clutter from amassing is to avoid all'open and "exposed" furniture; you have to get containers, wardrobes and furniture with doors, which eventually allow you to temporarily "hide" the disorder.

The other secrets to keeping chaos out are:

Establish rules, such as always putting things away in the place and in the way they were found;

Throw away anything you don't need or arrange to donate it to someone who might need it;

Distribute cleaning and tidying over time, avoiding doing everything together.

As a final trick, the psychologist recommends adding a pinch of fun; while you tidy up the house you can put on some music or turn on the comedy program you like best!

CHAPTER 4 WHY TIDYING UP AND CLEANING THE HOUSE MAKES US SO HAPPY

A clean and tidy home contributes to our emotional and mental well-being.

Tidying up and cleaning the house can make us happier. Indeed, there is nothing more relaxing and satisfying than entering an organized home, where a kind of peace and calm reigns. But have you ever wondered why this happens? According to scientific and psychiatric studies, a clean home also contributes to our emotional and mental well-being.

All experts agree that a little discipline and order can work as therapy and contribute to a happier life. How?

Reduces anxiety

Swati Mittal, a consultant psychiatrist for Fortis Noida and Swastik Assist Homes, says that, in addition to burning calories, our body releases endorphins and chemicals that make us feel good. This means that these types of activities can reduce anxiety and positively contribute to our mental health.

Increase happiness

"An orderly and organized environment affects our mental and physical state in ways we cannot imagine. From having more family time to creating a stress-free life, good organization contributes to a happier life," confirms Gayatri Gandhi, organizer by profession.

Improve concentration and performance

The feeling of living in a clean environment also increases confidence and provides a sense of satisfaction and motivation. "If our environment is in order, so will we be, and we will perform better," says psychiatrist Jinesh Shah.

Cleanup and the pandemic

Jinesh Shah recalls that "focusing on cleaning and disinfecting surfaces during the pandemic was stressful and created anxiety for many people." Stressing, "The pandemic has had a particularly negative impact on people with OCD who are obsessed with cleanliness, as it has aggravated their symptoms."

Here's a tip: We should never ignore cluttered spaces, unsanitary living conditions, poor personal hygiene or a listless approach to life, "as it is a clear sign of depression that requires immediate medical attention."

CHAPTER 5 COUPLES ARE CLOSER AND HAPPIER IN A CLEAN AND TIDY HOUSE

The holidays are over; putting everything back in its place was challenging and, little by little, we resume the daily routine, made up of a daily dose of order and organization. Many couples do not find the balance between household chores and personal needs.

Some experts suggest dedicating at least half an hour a day to tidying up the house, but not everyone is able to make that time or maybe get up earlier in the morning to dedicate themselves to their nest. Yet, it is enough to imagine the pleasure of returning to a loved and tidy home to already feel involved.

Have you already experienced the pleasure of sharing the daily chores as a couple?

In reality, a few tricks, organized and divided, are enough and everything will magically flow faster. From the bedroom to the bathroom, without neglecting the kitchen and what was not put away the night before, a healthy couple organization will allow us to leave the house ready for our return.

If as soon as you wake up, before escaping to the bathroom, we open the bedroom window for just 5 minutes, we are already doing a small fundamental action: ventilating! Removing germs and bacteria re-oxygenates the room and protects us from allergies. In addition, leaving the bed open to let out the humidity allows you to find it healthier in the evening. A few minutes and, making the bed together, it will seem that we have already carried out a first important task to bring order to the room with our partner.

If one of the two is dedicated to preparing breakfast, the other can arrange the living room, tidying up the blankets, pillows and other things left around, the trick is to start with what catches the eye first and then focus on the details.

After sharing breakfast, the ideal is to do the washing up, it will only take a few seconds, and while one partner washes, the other can dry next to them, also drying the sink and taps.

A tidy kitchen makes you want to use it ... when you return. The complicity of these small gestures could give a different profile to your days, the pleasure of sharing these little things with order and organization takes a few precious moments that make our daily life richer and more powerful.

A few more minutes and together in the bathroom, folding the towels, leaving nothing lying around, putting everything away in the cabinets is a small measure to make the room even cleaner, drying the sink and taps here too.

Leaving the bulk of the work to do together for the weekend, seeing a tidier home will put us at ease when we return.

When, giving yourself a pat on the back, you turn to look at the beautiful and welcoming house that awaits you, you will be proud to have made, together with your partner, those little attentions that will make you happy to return later.

CHAPTER 6 ON DECLUTTERING

How to declutter: the secrets of this real philosophy of life.

Decluttering is not the simple elimination of unnecessary objects: it is a real attitude oriented towards the essentials. A liberation that opens up the future and new possibilities.

When avoiding the dust becomes an obstacle course and finding something in a cabinet almost a mission impossible, then comes the time to get rid of unnecessary items: declutter, and "eliminate what clutters".

In Anglo-Saxon countries this practice has now become a true philosophy of life: selecting and eliminating what is no longer used, in fact, seems to have a real benefit also on an inner level, "freeing us" from the past, opening our minds to the future and to new possibilities.

Owning less to live better: is this perhaps the secret of happy degrowth? Given this ethically correct assumption, putting it into practice is a different matter, let's see some tips.

Decluttering: practical advice

Let's start with space cleaning, or how to reorganize spaces and, consequently, your life.

The experts advise drawing up a "ranking" of the rooms with the more messy spaces, in an orderly fashion, and focus on one area at a time.

You should do a "scan" of the objects, wondering how many times you have used them in the last 12 months: if you realize you have never used them, it is time to get rid of them.

The selection of objects, of course, must be made according to eco-sustainable principles.

They must therefore be separated carefully to differentiate them in the garbage, while what can be "saved" instead, can be sold or bartered.

If you are not ready to get rid of the objects immediately, keep them in a box and give yourself a period of tim. If after the period you realize you have never used it, it is really time to throw it away.

The excuse of "I don't have time" does not apply: once you have chosen the room to tidy up you can dedicate half an hour a day to decluttering, or just one day of the weekend, depending on your availability.

Decluttering: how to proceed.

Thankfully, decluttering experts provide good advice for every circumstance.

Take 5 minutes a day.

Throw away one item a day.

Use a garbage bag: you will be amazed at the speed with which it will fill up with objects you thought you could not part with.

Compile a list of the zones / rooms to be cleaned, starting with the simplest: proceed one zone at a time, crossing it off the list.

Apply the 12-12-12 scheme, drawing up a list with 12 things to throw away, 12 to donate and 12 to return to their rightful owners: tidying up in this way will be more fun and less traumatic!

Change perspective to see your home in a new light, perhaps by taking photos of your home before and after decluttering.

Experiment with numbers, for example wearing the same 33 items of clothing for 3 months: the aim is to understand that you can live with fewer things.

When you really have a hard time separating yourself from something, try asking yourself 'If I bought it today how much would I be willing to pay for it?'

Use the 'four boxes' technique: when you have to tidy up a room, get 4 boxes and write on them 'TO THROW, TO DONATE, TO KEEP, TO REUSE', and then you will have to choose which box to put each item in; the procedure can be long, but it works!

For those items that you don't want to throw away, you can apply 3 simple 'storage' rules.

Make a selection of the chosen objects, dividing them by year or by period (old house, university, etc.).

Keep children's objects in a dedicated container and place them inside the wardrobe, where they are not cluttered: when you want, you can always take them to look for something.

Develop a functional archiving method: your children's clothes and photos, for example, can be stored in folders or albums, or you can digitize them and store them in digital folders.

We now come to the "hot" area of this period: the wardrobe. In spring and autumn, it is time for seasonal changes: let's make the most of them to tidy up our clothes and, why not, our lives. You know, deciding what to keep and what to throw away is always difficult, but with some ad hoc advice everything will be easier.

The 4 boxes rule also applies to clothes: to keep, to file, to donate, to throw away. Throw away the clothes only if you have no alternatives, otherwise do everything possible to reuse them in some way, for example organizing a barter market with friends.

A useful trick to select clothes is this: hang the dubious clothes in the opposite direction to the others, or make a mark on the hangers. Only when / if you wear the garment can you turn the hanger correctly or remove the mark. At the end of the season, garments that have never been used must be eliminated.

Throw away damaged or useless hangers, then divide the remaining ones by placing similar ones next to each other: in this way the visual impact will be better.

After the difficult selection phase, clean the inside of the wardrobe thoroughly: vacuum the bottom and dust shelves and other surfaces.

The operation is tiring, but it will pay off: seeing the wardrobe in order will make you feel lighter.

The important thing is to maintain discipline even afterwards, avoiding starting to fill it with useless items on the first shopping trip.

CHAPTER 7 THROWING AWAY THE SUPERFLUOUS

How to get rid of unnecessary things for the house: to tidy your life and learn to throw away the superfluous.

Eliminating the superfluous in the house is essential, if we do not want to find ourselves buried alive by all the objects and clothes we no longer use. However, it is not always easy to get rid of unnecessary things, indeed, for many people it is very difficult.

Some objects, although devoid of material utility, are full of precious memories and it is normal not to want to get rid of them. Many of these memories, however, lie forgotten for years in the bottom of a drawer, with the sole purpose of taking up space. Therefore, we must learn to select the things that actually should not be thrown away and those that, instead, should end up in the trash immediately. Here are 10 ways, techniques and lifestyles to do it.

10 ways to get rid of unnecessary items in the house.

• Organize your work. Tidying up the whole house, from the bedroom to the pantry, in a single day is impossible and counterproductive. It is advisable to set dates in a cleaning calendar, dividing the work into several days, so as not to miss anything.

• Don't buy new things. If you always buy and don't want to throw anything away, the best thing to do is to stop shopping, which obviously increases the things you have at home.

• Ask for help. If not enough time to do the cleaning, ask relatives and friends for help. To save space, Marie Kondo's videos can also help.

• Fill boxes. If there are things that just can't be thrown away, put them in boxes, and then store them in the garage or basement so that they leave more space in the house. Maybe the following year will be the right time to throw them away for good.

• Throw away the things you don't use. To make clean break, things and clothes that have not been used for a long time could be thrown away. There should be no regrets, as your tastes, perhaps, may have changed over time.

• Organize papers and documents. Keeping all documents is important, but often unnecessary paper ends up in the middle. It is therefore necessary to buy folders or binders with labels to keep the important things aside. The rest is to be thrown into the paper bin.

• Tidy up the pantry. When you go to the supermarket you always end up buying useless products, which end up expiring. Check the expiration dates, in order to consume the food in the right time, avoiding waste.

• Give to charity. Give the old clothes, (in good condition that you don't wear) to the poor and needy. You have to put them all in bags and boxes (making sure they are not too worn) and take them to the associations that deal with these things. Surely in your neighborhood there will also be a parish church or an association that collects used clothes for the needy.

• Save space. A good thing is to keep the house in order, so that you can find all the things you are looking for in a short time, and avoid forgetting that you have them.

• Make selections. Obviously, there are objects that you can't help but keep, because they symbolize moments in your life and create a memory. It is advisable to try to understand which are the most important objects, and the others that remain must be thrown away.

CHAPTER 8 100 USELESS THINGS TO THROW AWAY

We often have no idea how many useless objects are clogging up our rooms: here is a super useful list of useless things compiled by a space-clearing expert.

In recent years, the fashion of "decluttering" and "space clearing" have haunted us, but even if you don't like Marie Kondo, admit that having a house that is always tidy and with few objects to manage is incredibly good for the soul.

After all, the organization of the house is a real science, and even if you can not detach yourself even from the objects you no longer use, you must admit that having more free space - in addition to being comfortable and making life easier - manages to give a certain serenity.

Beginning to declutter in general is not easy, also because we often and willingly touch much deeper chords: the objects we insist on keeping are often not simply "things", but often symbols we cling to. If you don't know how to do it, know that the most important step is the first. And to do that here is a list of objectively useless things that you can start eliminating right away.

Here is the list of 100 useless things that affect both our home and our life and that we mentally struggle to get rid of

1. Dry cleaning hangers

2. Newspapers from the day before

3. Unwanted emails

4. Remote controls that do not control anything

5. Sports gadgets

6. Worn Christmas decorations

7. Expired warranties and contracts

8. Tablecloths, too large or too small

9. Mismatched socks

10. Email addresses you don't recognise

11. Broken spatulas and tools

12. Sachets of condiments

13. Empty cans, jars and bottles

14. History on the computer

15. Planters you don't use

16. Fake friends on Facebook

17. Jigsaw puzzles with missing pieces

18. Wedding gifts you don't use

19. Unused stuffed animals

20. Bad photographs

21. Unnecessary business cards

22. Difficult and laborious recipes

23. Fax machines

24. Baggy dresses

25. Manuals for item you no longer have

26. Pagers

27. Vacation memories you don't like

28. Dead plants

29. Newsletters you don't read

30. Stained, torn or frayed towels

31. Dry pens and markers

32. Food leftovers

33. Old video game accessories

34. Obsolete video games

35. Duplications of digital photographs

36. Recorded TV series you will never watch

37. Notebooks that are no longer needed

38. Too much underwear ... (we understand each other!)

39. Shopping bags of paper or plastic

40. Store catalogs now available online

41. e-books that you will not re-read

42. Ruined sweaters

43. Keys without locks

44. Chipped or damaged tableware

45. Sunglasses you don't use

46. Old school materials

47. Dry paint cans

48. Cooler bags that are too small, large or heavy

49. Shoe boxes

50. Birthday decorations

51. Uncomfortable or broken earphones

52. Invitations to past events

53. Passwords no longer in use

54. Silver jewelry you no longer wear (sell it!)

55. Broken electronic appliances

56. Stationery unused in the past 3 months

57. Cable channels (choose fewer and pay less)

58. Expired discount coupons

59. Umbrellas that don't open or that hold the wind

60. Toys for animals now unusable

61. Ugly fridge magnets

62. Trash in the computer trash can

63. Unused flower pots

64. Commitments dated on the calendar

65. Scraps of fabric

66. Cables for audio and video equipment

67. Yellow Pages

68. Paperback books you won't re-read

69. Requests for donations and charities

70. Gold jewelry you never wear (sell it!)

71. Empty candy and gift boxes

72. Useless mail

73. Trophies from your childhood

74. Cookbooks you've never used

75. Twitter contacts that communicate too much

76. Pool toys

77. Old greeting cards

78. Pajamas you don't like

79. Tourist brochures

80. Industrial foods that you do not consume

81. Stained clothes

82. Apps you don't use

83. Shoes that hurt you

84. Used plastic cups

85. Glass covers

86. Doubles of class photos

87. Car fluids that are no longer needed

88. Magazines more than three months old

89. Clotted nail polish

90. Shopping receipts

91. Shoe laces for shoes you no longer have

92. Broken or ignored toys

93. Worn doormats

94. Pins on Pinterest you don't need

95. Dishes you never use

96. Wallpaper you no longer have on the walls

97. Old pillows

98. Obsolete mobile phones

99. Bottle caps

100. Ducklings for the bath that are no longer used

The 5 "NOTs" of the superfluous object

How to know if you can get rid of something without repenting? Geralin Thomas proposes the strategy of the 5 nots. An object is to be thrown away if it falls into one of these cases:

1. You don't use it.

2. You don't want it.

3. You don't love him.

4. You have not decided or chosen.

5. You have not completed it and therefore cannot use it (applies, for example, to do-it-yourself items).

CHAPTER 9 HOW TO GET RID OF CLUTTER

The best way to keep a clean and organized home is to get rid of things that are no longer needed. Clutter can be detrimental to your home life, if only to make it easy to find things when you need them. Most of us tend to keep objects even if we have not used them for a long time, either because they recall an emotional bond, or for prudence in cases of economic difficulty, or for simple inertia. It is a wise thing to break free from old things to make room for new ones.

Part 1: Collect Things

This first part describes how to find and rearrange things. Don't waste time wondering what to do with newly recovered things; if their use is evident immediately, fix them, otherwise put them in the sorting piles.

1

Check all items that are outdated or no longer usable. Be brutal. If they clutter up the room, and you no longer have a normal place to live, put them in the pile to tidy up later. After all, do you really need those magazines you've been collecting since 1998 but rarely read?

2

Empty the closet and all drawers. Take any clothes that no longer fit you or are out of fashion now, and put them in the sorting pile.

3

Gather together all the sheets of paper and various documents that you have scattered around. Recycle or throw away the ones you don't need. Keep the rest in organized folders.

4

First clean up any places that attract clutter, such as the bed. Then remove all objects from this area. Throw out the things you no longer need, clean up the dirty ones, and put everything else back in its place. Anything you don't know whether to keep goes in the sorting pile.

Part 2: Order

1

Put the sorting pile in a large clean area so you can see everything to organize the tidying up well.

2

Ask yourself the three basic questions about the objects that ended up in the pile:

Do you like it?

Do you use it often, or will you use it soon (within 3 months)?

Will you miss it when you get rid of it? Is it a very important memory for you?

3

Divide the pile into three distinct groups.

First group: the things you use almost every day and the things you "like".

For example, the telephone, tools, shoes, and so on. You can put the keys in a bowl near the door, you can keep the tools in a toolbox, or buy yourself a shoe cabinet. Find any solution that works for you and helps you find all the most important items with ease.

The things you are attached to, such as photos, knick-knacks, etc ... should now find a place to display them or keep them hidden, or keep them carefully, etc ...

Second group: Here you should put the things you use at least once a week or once a month. These are generally items that should be kept in closets, garages, or other out-of-the-way places. Reorder them in containers (better if they are transparent, so you can easily see the contents) and label them. Other things, like clothes, put them away on hangers.

Third group: should include things you haven't used for at least six months or a year. If you haven't used them in all this time, chances are you won't use them any more. So, get rid of them forever. Give all the items you don't use or no longer want to charities, so that they can be used by someone less fortunate.

4

Don't think you can tidy everything up in one day. Depending on how much mess there is, it could take two days or a week. If it's emotionally demanding, it may take months, and it's a good idea to call a friend or objective mate to help you morally as well.

Advice

Try tidying up one room at a time. Start from one corner and arrange it in your own style and arrange the whole room before moving on to the next one.

Treat yourself to a movie in the cinema, a new dress, or a trip once you're done. Rewards can help you get on with the project, giving you an incentive to complete the task.

If you need to tidy up after work, try doing it a little at a time. Take fifteen minutes each night to tackle a small area, drawer, or shelf.

You can donate items to charities. It could be old clothes, old shoes, old toys, old appliances, etc ...

Keep order! Working 15 minutes a day to fix a room is better than spending days tidying up a house every year or so. Remember that any improvement is better than nothing. If you get tired, take a five-minute break and then go back to work. You can listen to some music while you are busy for an hour or two.

Set a specific time to reorder. Never try to do this after a long day at work if you can avoid it.

If you live in Australia, you can enter the things you no longer need in "Free Treasure", www.freetreasure.com.au and find someone who comes to pick them up at your home; so you save time finding other things to get rid of.

Warnings

Don't try to rearrange an entire house in one day.

Before starting the task, make sure you have the energy and time to complete it. A good rule of thumb is not to take out more than you can tidy up in an hour. Set a timer for one hour, and when it's over, you can decide whether to work for another hour if you have the strength. Give yourself a 15- or 20-minute break as a reward, look at emails, have a cup of tea, or lie down on the sofa.

Remember that there is a difference between clutter and objects that create the atmosphere and environment of the areas you clean. This distinction depends on the person.

You can ask friends or relatives for help. But don't call a friend who has the soul of a junk dealer, or you will find yourself in a worse situation. And be careful not to ask for help from someone who is too tidy. If you try to get rid of all your "precious" items you could panic and end up throwing nothing away!

Don't force yourself to tidy up. Make it pleasant, or you will soon lose interest. Trust the progress you can make. You can't think of tidying up the mess, that has formed over a long time, overnight.

CHAPTER 10 ORGANIZING THE HOUSE: THE 30-DAY CHALLENGE

Blogger Ashlina Kaposta has devised a 30-day challenge to become real "domestic gods" in one month.

The purpose of this month-long commitment is to make the home more welcoming and tidier with minimal daily effort and, at the invitation of @thedecorista, to share your progress with her on Instagram with the hashtag #domesticbliss30.

This kind of challenge, especially if not too long, as in this case, can be a solution to organize life at home step by step and make changes constant over time.

Here are the daily commitments proposed:

Day 1 - Assess the situation

The blogger suggests setting some goals and drawing up a top 5 of the areas of the house that are in urgent need of refurbishment.

Day 2 - Get rid of the paper

Raise your hand if your house is not full of paper, old documents and receipts. It's time to throw away what you no longer need or put your important documents in containers and folders.

Day 3 - Aromatherapy

Diffusers, essential oils, incense: being greeted by a good scent when entering the house is essential.

Day 4 - Arrange the bathroom

Bathroom hygiene is a daily necessity, but dedicate a day entirely to this, from top to bottom. In addition to cleaning, it also takes care of order: the time has come to throw away unused samples, expired creams and broken hairpins in the drawers.

Day 5 - Clean the windows

Windows, mirrors, frames glass: spray everything mercilessly (if possible, with ecological methods, such as water and vinegar).

Day 6 - Put the books away

Organize your library, but that's not all. Gather the books scattered around the house, those on the nightstand for months or the titles left in the bathroom bin that you never read because magazines are faster...

Day 7 - Arrange the sofa

In other words: give shape to the cushions, fold any blankets in an orderly way and refresh the fabrics.

Day 8 - Starting the top 5

Review the 5 goals drawn up on day 1 and start implementing the first on the list.

Day 9 - Arrange the refrigerator

As with the bathroom, again it's time to throw out old sauces, come up with a recipe for things that are about to expire, and clean up all the shelves.

Day 10 - A touch of green

A house without plants is a sad house: adopt a floor plan. If you don't have a green thumb, you can start with succulents or hardy houseplants like Sansevieria, Ficus and Zamia.

For each type of plant, even if not delicate, find out about its needs for watering, natural light, soil.

Day 11 - Make the bed

Making your bed every day is a good aim, but if you usually can't, today is the time to get serious.

Put on clean sheets and try to make it perfect, better than you would ever find in a hotel.

Day 12 - Landfill drawers

We all have at least one: free the drawers from all the junk accumulated over the years.

Day 13 - Clean the light fittings

Uncomfortable and boring, but every now and then, like today, it has to be done.

Day 14 - Arrange your shoes

If the shoe rack is not enough, you can take advantage of the space under the bed or resort to practical DIY solutions.

Day 15 - Take a photo

Recreate a corner of the house that you like best in the style you prefer, photograph it and then share it. It doesn't have to be perfect but it has to reflect your tastes.

Day 16 - Plan a dinner

For you, for your loved one or for friends. The important thing is that every detail is perfect: turn off the TV, light the candles and... enjoy your meal!

Day 17 - Same as day 8

Review the 5 goals drawn up on day 1 and start implementing the second and third on the list.

Day 18 - Personality

Unleash your personality and make the house represent you. Express yourself through a DIY job, a decoration, a message on the bathroom mirror!

Day 19 - Set up a studio

Or in any case a corner of the house where you usually get to work, both as a profession and as a hobby. After tidying up, getting to work will be more pleasant.

Day 20 - The coffee table

Arrange any magazines left there for months, throw away anything that survived the apocalypse of day 2 and embellish it with a nice tray or an elegant book.

Day 21 - Adding fabrics

All it takes is a new pair of colorful curtains, an upholstered pillow, an IKEA fabric. Take a look here to light up the home with textiles.

Day 22 - The drinks trolley

Even if you don't drink alcohol, insert a corner dedicated to refreshment at home, perhaps for coffee or tea.

Day 23 - Same as day 8

Review the 5 goals drawn up on day 1 and start implementing the fourth and fifth on the list.

Day 24 - New prints

Almost every home has an abandoned picture that has been waiting for its call for months, if not years. If, on the other hand, you have nothing to hang and you have no creative flair, take a trip on the internet, find a design you like, print it and frame it. A simple and clean effect, to be used in a corner of the house with empty walls.

Day 25 - Welcome guests

Organize a small reception and invite friends or relatives. Tell us about your 30-day challenge and show the changes made so far.

Day 26 - Change of scenery

In the morning open all the windows of the house, weather permitting, light a few candles and perfume the rooms. It will bring new energy and everything will immediately seem cleaner and fresher.

Day 27 - Creating a personal space

Carving out a corner of your own at home is a gift that everyone should give themselves, regardless of the space available.

All it takes is a comfortable chair in a corner with a soft cushion, ten minutes of time, a good book and a coffee to start the day in a different way.

Day 28 - Fix up the garage

If not available, the cellar or any space used as a pantry. For some garages and boxes, it would take more than a day to fix everything, but try to do what you can.

Day 29 - A gift for the home

Go out and buy a small gift for your home. After all this work, you deserve it!

Day 30 - Final thoughts

The challenge is over. Appreciate what you have done this month and, why not, thank your house.

CHAPTER 11 HOW TO ORGANIZE THE KITCHEN

A disorganized kitchen can make your life very difficult! Knowing where to find what you need in the blink of an eye saves you time and unnecessary stress. Before starting to rearrange it, divide the various objects according to use. Then arrange the shelves and organize the drawers and furniture. Finally, try to make more space if there are other products to store.

Part 1 Divide Articles

1

Eliminate unnecessary items. If the drawers are full of stuff, you won't be able to find what you need. Do not keep bulky and unused items. To determine if you need something, consider the last time you used it, if it is still in good condition, and if you have duplicates. Give unused items to a friend or to charity. If you have accumulated tons of items that you no longer want or need, consider organizing a sale in front of your house.

Maybe you want to keep some kitchen utensils you don't use often, such as party dinnerware. If you don't have enough space to store them in the kitchen, it's best to find somewhere else.

2

Clean the kitchen from top to bottom. Dust the external surfaces of cabinets, appliances and any furnishings. Use a soapy rag and a clean, dry cloth to wash and dry the inside and outside of furniture and counter tops. Sweep and wash the floor. Wash and dry any rugs or other fabric items you have in the kitchen.

Your goal is to start from scratch! Since you are removing everything in the furniture and drawers, this is the best time to clean them. It is also not recommended to put dishes and appliances on top of a layer of dust and grime!

Expert Advice

Don't forget the fridge! Donna Smallin Kuper, an expert in home organization, advises: "When you want to thoroughly clean your refrigerator, remove everything from the shelves, including any removable drawers. Use an all-purpose cleaning spray and a microfiber cloth to wipe the shelves one at a time, starting with the top one. Wash the removable parts with warm soapy water, rinse and dry them, and put them back in the refrigerator. Finally, put back the food you removed from the appliance."

3

Establish work stations. Choose them based on how you use the kitchen. This will make it easier to decide which zone to put the current in. Here are some ideas:

Coffee or tea station: place the coffee maker or kettle in an easily accessible spot. Keep cups and mugs nearby.

Food Processing Station: create enough space to prepare food. Keep the cutting board, knives, measuring cups and everything you need close at hand.

Cooking station: in other words, it rotates around the hob. Keep crockery nearby, but also pot holders and oven mitts.

Station to Serve: If you have space, you may include a point where you put the food on the plates. Choose a free shelf and keep the necessary utensils, such as the ladle and skimmer, close at hand.

4

Choose accessible places for the items you use most often. You should take them, use them, wash them and replace them easily. Keep them close at hand or near the dishwasher, sink or stove. Avoid stacking pots and pans on top of each other, or you'll have to rummage around to find what you need.

5

Group similar objects together. Sort them by category, such as glasses, pots, cutlery and containers. By storing them in the same place, it will be easier to find what you need.

Eliminate duplicates or things you don't use.

Part 2 Organize the Shelves

1

Remove utensils that you rarely use from the shelves. For example, you could leave the microwave oven if you use it every day and store the toaster if you only use it once a week.

2

Place appliances and the most useful items on the kitchen counter. Identify areas that need to remain empty, such as the food preparation station. Then, choose a spot for the dishes and appliances you need on a daily basis, such as the microwave oven, coffee pot, dish drainer, and cutting board.

Check where the power outlets are before deciding where to place the small appliances.

3

Place the kitchen utensils you use most in a container near the stove. These are the ladle, the spatula, the spoon for serving spaghetti and the skimmer. Put only the ones you use most often and keep in a drawer the ones you use most rarely.

A large jar or container is ideal for these tools.

4

Install a magnetic bar to hang knives. Put the others in a drawer.

Give away the knife block and unused knives.

5

Arrange the hand soap and sponges. Place a small tray near the sink to save space. Put on hand soap, dish sponge, and dish towel. Then, place the sink stopper and bottle cleaning brush lower.

You can buy a shelf to install over the kitchen sink. Alternatively, use your wits and use a cake stand for storage!

6

Place the oil and honey on a plate or tray. Furthermore, residues can settle inside the furniture and on the shelves, getting greasy and greasing other objects! Place them on a saucer or tray or tray that you can easily wash.

7

Group the fruit and vegetables in a basket or bowl.

Part 3 Organize Furniture and Drawers

1

Assign each cabinet and drawer to a category. So, arrange everything as you have decided. Put the items you use most often towards the front for easy picking. By grouping them by category, you can quickly find everything you need.

Put the dishes in a large cabinet, the glasses in a less spacious cabinet, the pots and pans in a low cabinet, and so on.

A drawer for tea towels and pot holders, another for cutlery and another for less used kitchen utensils

2

Keep kitchen cleaning products under the sink.

3

Use trays with compartments to organize drawers.

4

Arrange items on small, easy-to-remove trays to keep the furniture tidy. You can put them on the top shelf of the furniture

5

Place dry foods in clear containers for easy identification. Place them in special containers to eliminate clutter and keep the pantry organized. Pour the grains, flour, and ingredients for making desserts into stackable bowls. Then, arrange them nicely in the cupboards.

Group them by categories. For example, put the cereals together, collect the packets of pasta and gather the ingredients for cakes.

6

Organize the lids and baking sheets. Get a separator or magazine rack and place it inside the cabinet, then insert the lids and trays. Opt for a sturdy metal separator so that it stands upright.

To store these kitchen utensils, either a plastic or a metal magazine rack will work.

7

Use a turntable so you don't have to rummage around the cabinet for what you need.

8

Keep the junk drawer tidy by using small resealable containers. If you have a drawer in which you store a disparate set of items, optimize the space by arranging everything in small boxes. Label them so that you recognize what you put inside.

Check the contents regularly and get rid of unused items.

Part 4 Fill the refrigerator

1

Put ready-to-eat food and drinks on the top shelf. They include prepackaged foods, eggs and leftovers. The upper shelf is the one to be accessed more easily. Furthermore, by placing these foods in the upper part of the refrigerator, you will prevent them from contaminating the dishes placed on the lower levels. Arrange bottles too high for the top shelf on the middle shelf. Avoid putting them in the door area as it is not very cold.

2

Store the meat on the bottom shelf. This will prevent blood from dripping and contaminating other foods. However, make sure it is closed properly before placing it in the refrigerator, otherwise it could spread bacteria. If it leaks anywhere, pack it up again and clean the area with an antibacterial cleanser.

Place the meat in a container, even if it leaks, it will not end up contaminating the vegetables.

3

Store your fruit and vegetables on the center shelf or in the drawer. However, it is preferable to store them in the drawer as it hinders moisture and provides a better environment for these foods.

If you're using the drawer, make sure you don't overfill it.

4

Put the seasonings on the door shelves. Group them by genre to easily find what you need.

For example, combine jams and marmalades, group the marinades and put all the sauces to season sandwiches in one place.

5

Put the cheeses and cold cuts in the cheese drawer.

Part 5 Create more space

1

Use the space above the wall cabinets or the refrigerator. Do not leave the top surfaces unused. Use them to store items you don't use often. You can also take unused dishes to the basement.

Use the furthest (and least practical) surfaces to place knick-knacks.

You could use the space above the wall units to put knick-knacks or things you don't need.

2

Use a trolley if you have limited space in furniture. You can buy it at a mall, home improvement store, or on the Internet.

3

Use a shelf without doors for easy access. It can contain other dishes, small appliances that you use little, dry ingredients, recipe books and knick-knacks. Choose a kitchen wall and hang it or, if space is limited, place it on the side of the refrigerator. Arrange the objects with taste and harmony.

A shelf is perfect because it is practical and graceful at the same time!

4

Add some shelves. It is a great way to increase storage space. You can also use plastic foldable shelves. You can buy them at a mall, home improvement store, or on the Internet.

5

Install hooks on the walls or inside the cabinet doors. Attach them to the hob wall or over the sink. Mount them inside the furniture for hanging small objects. They can be used to hang pots and pans, decorations, measures, tea towels and so on.

6

Consider a fabric shoe rack to hang on the pantry door. The smaller pockets are perfect for keeping an eye on many small items. If you prefer, you can also add labels.

7

Buy a kitchen island with casters for storage and cooking. Being equipped with wheels, it can be moved comfortably according to the needs of those who use it. It will give you more space not only to prepare your dishes, but also to store utensils in the drawers, cabinets or on the open shelves at the bottom.

Sizes vary as well as prices: you can find cheap models, but also expensive ones. You can buy it at furniture and home improvement stores or on the Internet.

8

Install drawers in low cabinets to maximize space. If you want you can try to build them yourself or get help from a carpenter.

Advice

You may want to try various arrangements until you find the right one. Consider what makes your life easier and what you don't need.

If you have a "junk drawer", check the contents often to make sure you don't store any unused items. Even if the junk drawer is useless and should be eliminated, this way you gain space and get rid of the junk. That slimming herbal tea that has been there for 10 years and that you have never tried. The fillet recipe you never dared to cook. The piece of an old blender you have long since thrown away. Of all these things the best solution is: throw.

Organize everything you need in the kitchen according to your actual needs, not according to an "ideal" trend in domestic life.

Warnings

Before buying containers and shelves for kitchen organization, review all the items and try to figure out if you want to keep them or need to make a selection. If you buy something you don't really need, the clutter will tend to increase.

CHAPTER 12 CLEAN THE HOUSE NATURALLY

You can clean the house effectively and quickly, using natural products such as vinegar, denatured alcohol and more. Let's find out how.

The house is the place where we spend the most hours of the day, so it is important to take care of it, cleaning and disinfecting it in depth. It can also be done without the use of chemicals which are most often very aggressive.

The house can be cleaned with products that you certainly have available, such as white wine vinegar, bicarbonate of soda and many others, let's find out how to use them best.

1-White wine vinegar

White wine vinegar is a widely used product especially for cleaning the house. It can be defined as an ally for women, which can replace commercial products that most of the time contain too aggressive substances. The combination of vinegar with citric or lemon acid and bicarbonate enhances its effectiveness. Mixed with hydrogen peroxide, it manages to achieve even more incredible results. In particular, you can use vinegar in the kitchen and in the bathroom, let's find out how.

In the kitchen, you can degrease the oven, just pour a mixture of water and vinegar on a sponge. If the oven is very dirty and gives off an unpleasant smell, try this; in a spray bottle, put 4 tablespoons of salt, with a glass of vinegar, mix and steam directly in the oven. It is recommended to leave it on for 15 minutes, then clean with a soft sponge. Clean the fridge, after having emptied it and disconnected the power, prepare a mixture of water and vinegar, dip a sponge or microfiber cloth and wash well.

It also eliminates stains and sanitizes the gas hob, also try to clean the taps, sinks and kitchen surfaces, perhaps put the mixture of water and vinegar in a spray bottle.

If you often smell an unpleasant smell in the kitchen and bathroom, the problem could be with the drains and plumbing of the sinks. When the smell is persistent, it could spread throughout the house.

The solution to the problem can be mitigated with vinegar combined with bicarbonate. Put 1/2 liter of water to boil in a saucepan, then add about 200 ml of vinegar, in the meantime pour about 100 g of sodium bicarbonate inside the pipe giving off the bad odor. Then pour the water with vinegar into the pipe, you will have an effervescent reaction, which is completely normal. If you follow this advice, you will reduce the bad smell. Routine maintenance is important.

In the bathroom, however, vinegar can disinfect surfaces and taps, proceed as for the kitchen, prepare a solution of water and vinegar and put it in a spray bottle and spray in the tub or shower, to eliminate dirt or soap residues. In case of limescale stains or bad smell from the toilet, pour in vinegar and leave it to act, then pour in buckets of hot water.

Vinegar is perfect to eliminate the mold on tiles or shower curtain, just put a little bit of water and vinegar on a soft sponge and clean.

2-Tea tree oil

Tea tree oil is obtained from the distillation of the Malaleuca Alternifolia tree, widely used for both personal and home care. Known for its disinfectant properties, a real natural antibacterial. It is recommended for house cleaning especially if there are pets such as dogs and cats.

You can use it in different ways, cleaning ceramic, porcelain stoneware or terracotta floors, but not parquet. Just put 3 liters of warm water in a bucket, then add a glass of alcohol vinegar and 10 drops of tea tree oil. If you want to scent a little more, add 3 drops of lavender essential oil.

Clean both kitchen and bathroom tiles, even if mold is present. Prepare a mixture of 4 glasses of distilled water with 20 drops of tea tree essential oil, a little baking soda and white vinegar. Spray on a microfiber cloth and clean. In case of more stubborn dirt, proceed in this way: spray directly on the tiles and let it act, then remove with a sponge and then clean with a soft cloth.

The hob burners are a real torture; it often happens that there is stubborn dirt, which is not easily removed. Create a pasty mixture with 5 tablespoons of baking soda and 7 drops of tea tree essential oil, apply the homogeneous solution. Leave it on for a few minutes and then gently remove the dirt with a sponge.

3-Eucalyptus oil

Eucalyptus oil brings many benefits, in fact it is often used for personal care. It is obtained from Eucalyptus globulus, a plant of the Mirtaceae family. Useful for treating seasonal ailments and more, including colds, headaches, cystitis and sinusitis. But this oil can be used to clean the house, disinfecting it in a natural way, in fact it eliminates bacteria and germs. Just add 150 ml for every liter of water, then you can proceed with both the cleaning of the floors and the tiles.

4-Sodium bicarbonate

Sodium bicarbonate is a natural product, an ally for women, which can be used both for cleaning the house and for the person. But it is also used in the kitchen for the preparation of various recipes, especially for baked goods.

Bicarbonate was used by our grandmothers, it is known that it is an ecological detergent that not only deodorizes, whitens, but cleans deeply. It is called a natural disinfectant; it has the ability to eliminate bacteria and eliminates bad smells. In fact, it is often used in the fridge or oven. Let's examine in detail how to use it.

Does your fridge smell bad and you don't know how to stop it? It often happens that you open the fridge and smell a bad smell, but if you clean the fridge frequently, you can avoid the formation of unpleasant odors or mold.

Just put the baking soda and a little lemon juice in a glass. On the other hand, if the oven stinks, put water and baking soda in a bowl and create a pasty solution. Apply it to a sponge and clean the oven, even if the pans and pot have a bad smell.

Cleaning the tiles and floors can be done by mixing 2 tablespoons of baking soda in a bucket of hot water, then proceed with washing, if you want to give a little perfume, add the drops of essential oil to lavender or jasmine. Anything that smells bad can be treated with baking soda, even cat litter bins or litter boxes that often stink. Even ashtrays, after washing them, ifthey stink, put a little baking soda and let it act a little.

5-Denatured alcohol

Alcohol denatured at 90°, the one that has a pink color, can be used for house cleaning, just dilute it with water. It has the ability to break down a large number of viruses and bacteria, in no time, which is why it is an ally of women for cleaning the house. But in detail, what can be cleaned?

Floors and tiles, just pay attention because it is particularly flammable, dilute it in water and clean the surfaces with a soft cloth. Remember that in the case of parquet and terracotta floors, the use is not recommended.

As an alternative to these products, if you have a steam mop available, you can use that. In fact, the steam cleans and sanitizes all the surfaces of the house, thanks to the high temperatures, which are able to dissolve even the most stubborn dirt from floors, bathroom fixtures and tiles. In addition, the steam jet can also kill most of the germs and bacteria.

CHAPTER 13 10 HOME ORGANIZING IDEAS THAT WILL CHANGE YOUR LIFE

How many times do you happen to think: "I have to fix this, I have to fix that, but then you postpone it to the next day and you never do it.

Stop postponing with our tips

1. Less is more

What I always say in my consultancy is: "If everything is important, nothing is important", if you underline everything, in the end you do not underline anything, because you do not give value and prominence to the objects you own. The time you spend looking for things is longer than you think you will save by avoiding reordering. So, the less you have the more time you save.

2. Making lists

Not everyone loves lists, I am strongly addicted to them, because they rationalize the thousand ideas that come to my mind, so making lists helps me to make order and space in my head. If you don't love them, you can use pre-defined templates, with the days of the week. Lists are useful for families larger than one person; it is a useful method for defining roles in the home and also educating children to discipline and order. You can also consider medium-term lists, for monthly or bi-monthly activities, such as cleaning windows, cleaning the oven, defrosting the freezer and fridge (or you can also rely on your common sense!).

3. Risers for shelves

If you have very high shelves, don't underestimate the power of risers, which allow you to create space above and below to organize the furniture.

4. Focus on one environment at a time

You often get discouraged before starting because you think there are too many things to do and therefore you don't even start. If you really want to tidy up your home, divide the spaces and focus on one at a time. Do not think about the overall disorder, otherwise you will never find the urge to tidy up. One piece of furniture at a time, one corner at a time, one room at a time. You will see, once started, you will never be able to stop! Start with the smallest room.

5. Documents, archive them!

Do not pile up documents on your desk or in the hallway cabinets. Throw away unnecessary mail and unnecessary documents. Arrange important documents in filing cabinets.

6. Do not pile your clothes on chairs

After changing, put your clothes back in the closets or drawers.

7. Reuse boxes

Once again, I come back to talking about boxes! If beautiful, use them for plastic food containers in the kitchen, or for medicines or for stationery. I always prefer the square ones to the round ones, depending on the use you can make of them. I know people who have used wine containers to hold their socks and underwear, a great choice!

8. Do not stack objects on the bedside table

Having the essentials close to where you sleep is important for sleep. Loading the bedside table with too much stuff does not allow you to rest well and always leaves you in trouble. Keep the bedside table with the essentials, the bedside lamp, the alarm clock, some decorations, but nothing more. Try not to keep too many books on the bedside table, even though you are reading several at a time (also because at least they do not act as a receptacle for dust).

CHAPTER 14 HOW TO ORGANIZE A CHILD'S BEDROOM IN 3 SIMPLE STEPS

With this guide we want to help you optimize the spaces in your child's bedroom which is often the least organized space in your home by far... but it doesn't have to be!

We'll start by eliminating all that is superfluous, making sure your child's bedroom spaces are tidier and more organized. Let's begin!

3 simple steps to organize a child's bedroom

Step 1: get rid of everything that does not work, and is not useful.

Before you can actually organize your child's bedroom, chances are you need to get rid of a few things. Organize everything in the room by dividing it into two groups: useful and not useful. You can involve your child in this process, or you can choose to go through everything independently but thanks to his help you will not risk throwing away something that is really dear or useful to him. You could also take advantage of this process by using it for educational purposes: everything that is no longer needed can be donated to other less fortunate children or young people or to organizations that take care of children and young people with any kind of discomfort.

Let's start with the clothes! Sort out your child's drawers and closet by putting aside any clothing that he no longer uses or that no longer fits him. Children grow up at a frenzied pace and I imagine you will find more than a few unwrapped dresses, jeans and t-shirts.

Remember to set aside clothing items to donate. Select them from those in good and excellent condition. You cannot donate worn or torn clothing. Imagine that they must be worn by other less fortunate children / teens and that they must be as intact as possible.

Get rid of the toys your child no longer plays with. Children often have far more toys than they need to have a happy childhood. Again, you can donate the toys to charities for children most in need. Look for the institution closest to you and go to deliver them. Don't throw them away!

Is the furniture in the room still useful? Did you keep your child's old crib by putting it in a corner of his room? If your baby sleeps in his own bed, there is no point in having a cot in the room. Get rid of it!

Evaluate all the furniture in your child's room and make sure it is functional. Try to replace or eliminate anything the baby doesn't need.

Step 2: Add storage space for items and clothing in the room

If general clearing of the superfluous has not been enough to make room, you should find space-saving solutions to better organize the room. It might be time to consider some new furniture solutions that allow you to make the room more spacious and organized!

Shelving

Using the height of the room to store your baby's belongings is an easy way to optimize space. From toys to books, video games to movies, many of your child's items can be stored on shelves. You can also use containers stacked on top of each other.

If the room has a very low ceiling, using shelves is not the ideal solution but it is still possible!

You can use the space under the bed for storage.

Another easy way to maximize space under your child's bed? Get him a container bed!

You can also think about buying a container bed so that you don't have to have the task of organizing everything into boxes and containers.

Step 3: Make room organization easier by focusing on one section at a time.

Once you've got rid of everything your child no longer needs and have optimized the space inside the room with shelves and boxes to hide under the bed, it's time to rearrange the space.

The easiest way to do it? Focus on specific areas by optimizing one at a time.

Tips for organizing your child's desk

Your child's desk probably serves primarily as a homework station. Just a few items on the desk (pencils, pens and notebooks) are enough to make it look messy.

Here are a couple of tips and tricks to help you keep your toddler's desk organized:

Use containers that can be attached to the wall to hold pencils, markers, crayons, and other materials. Thus, a portion of the free space on the desk will not be occupied. There are beautiful baskets for stationery on the market.

Help your child create an organized system with labels and stickers on the drawers. It will be easier for the child / kid to know where certain items go without leaving them on the desk.

Tips for organizing your baby's toys.

Your child will have more time to keep his room organized if he can easily find the toys he is looking for. By storing items in clear plastic containers, you can keep things organized and easily accessible for your little one. You can purchase plastic containers with separate compartments to attach labels to. If the child is too young and still cannot read, use adhesive images to make him understand where to put his objects according to their type.

Make keeping order in the room fun! If you can help your child see how to sort and organize his toys, he will be much more likely to adopt the directions you gave him as a game.

CHAPTER 15 5 TRICKS TO KEEP THE CHILDREN'S ROOM TIDY AND ORGANIZED

Keeping your children's bedroom tidy for a long time can be really difficult if you don't run for cover in time. First of all, it is wrong to think that the order of the bedroom is dictated only by the desire to have the house perfectly clean.

If you consider that children spend most of their time right in the bedroom, to ensure their safety and health it is essential that this environment is tidy and clean.

In fact, having a tidy children's room positively influences the mood of the little ones, making them more predisposed to calm and serenity, reducing the stress of parents.

It is therefore important to set rules, but even before being able to design a room that is basically functional and therefore easy to organize and order. Understanding how it is more practical to arrange the furniture inside the children's environment or which are the most suitable accessories to furnish it, can help to create a well-kept space.

Taking into account the characteristics of the bedroom and the needs of your children can direct you towards furnishing solutions that help create a welcoming and well-organized environment. It is also important that children are accustomed from an early age to taking care of their bedroom, involving them in its organization and tidying up.

Does all this seem unattainable to you? In reality you will see that with a few tricks, the bedroom can become a completely tidy and clean space.

1. Separate the spaces

The children in their bedroom carry out many different activities that are the cause, very often, of the much-hated disorder.

Separating the bedroom into defined areas, providing specific spaces to be allocated to each children's activity, will allow you to avoid the accumulation of objects scattered everywhere. Having a separate sleeping area from the play area helps children to identify the various areas and use them based on the activity they have to carry out.

This undoubtedly contributes to keeping the children's bedroom tidy, as well as to having a much more functional space.

Dividing the play area from the study area, for example, prevents children from getting distracted when they are busy with their homework. The same goes for the sleeping area, which must be organized in such a way as to reconcile sleep and certainly not to favor night-time gaming sessions.

With the furnishing ideas currently on the market, it is not difficult to organize the children's bedroom. Furthermore, by choosing companies that offer tailor-made solutions, it is even easier to customize and organize the bedroom.

Do not forget that it is important to arrange the bedroom furniture to make it not only more functional but also safer: for this reason, it is vital to choose quality products.

2. Choose space-saving and order- saving furniture

The organization of the bedroom space is the prerequisite for ensuring order.

Therefore, it is better to prefer furniture that is right for the environment they have to furnish and suitable for optimizing it as much as possible.

Therefore, choosing space-saving solutions for children's bedrooms is almost a must in order to offer an environment dedicated to children suitable for their different needs, without living in absolute chaos.

3. Choose large and organized closets

It is useful to organize your children's closet in order to find the clothes easily, but also so that they can be put away quickly and methodically. With a super-organized wardrobe, it is certainly easier to have a tidy and practical children's bedroom.

Once you have chosen the most suitable wardrobe model for the bedroom, you can customize its interior to make it functional both for you and especially for your children.

4. Boxes and containers for toys.

Are you now resigned to thinking that the place for toys is in every corner of the bedroom floor?

Given that having fewer games can be an advantage for children, we certainly cannot blame you for the fact that it is practically impossible to have them all perfectly put in place.

In reality it is possible, because if you organize the bedroom with special boxes and containers in which each toy can be easily stored, at the end of the day or when the children have finished playing, order can finally be achieved.

It can be useful to organize the different containers for toys by type, perhaps by applying labels, so as to immediately identify the box / container of the game you need and keep the children's bedroom always tidy.

5. Get the children to cooperate

You have to eliminate from your head the misconception that your children are unable to order their own room.

Children from an early age must be used to collaborating and must be involved in the activities necessary to order their bedroom. In this way they will grow with the awareness of being responsible for their own things and spaces.

You can establish a few but effective rules, here are a few:

- Put away the games once you have finished playing;
- Before starting another game / activity, put away the objects you have just used;
- Each object must have its precise place.

A neat children's room makes everyone happy

Tidying up your children's bedroom is certainly a source of stress, not to mention the rest of the house!

If you can start designing a bedroom that invites you to order, in a sense the bulk of the work is done. In fact, in this way everything will have its place and it will be easier for you to rearrange.

Furthermore, having the children's bedroom tidy helps to make them feel in a welcoming and reassuring environment. Disorder, on the other hand, is a source of agitation and restlessness in children who are thus prone to generate confusion in the disorder.

To avoid this, offer your children a furniture solution that allows you to organize the space in a chaos-proof way. Contact companies specializing in children's furniture and who have developed, over the years, a whole series of solutions for bedrooms that can satisfy parents and children, in order to make everyone happy.

This means choosing those who offer you functional and practical bedrooms as well as made with quality, resistant and non-toxic materials.

Remember again that it is essential for you to have the ability to customize the bedroom, so as to be able to organize the space to get the order you want.

Once you have furnished the bedroom and adopted all the solutions to prepare it in the best possible way, do not forget that it is important to educate your children and get them used to tidying up their bedroom.

After all, tidying up the bedroom can be a fun game to play with children, as well as useful for mom and dad.

CHAPTER 16 THE RIGHT PLACE FOR EVERY OBJECT

Is the mess driving you crazy? An organized lifestyle can make your days more productive and more relaxing at the same time. When your home is tidier, it will look cleaner and you will find that you have more space at your disposal, easy to use and exploit. Follow the tips in this guide to start organizing your home!

Part 1 Eliminate Useless Things

1

Put your items in order. Examine the things in each room, dividing them according to what you intend to do: choose what you want to keep, give and throw away. Keep the items you need and cannot be separated from; throw away completely useless things, which no one would use anymore; finally, give items to charity that you cannot use, but which may prove useful for someone else.

2

Evaluate the items to keep rationally. Sometimes one gets the impression of needing something even if it is not true, but it is this attitude that pushes us to accumulate objects, leaving little space for the really important things. Once you have established what to do with each item, examine the remaining ones, think back to the last time you used them and decide if you actually need them.

3

When you decide to give an item to charity, donate it to someone who would make good use of it. Choose the charity to donate it to based on the type of item (for example, toys to the Salvation Army, clothes to the parish, and so on). Make sure you throw away any unusable items. You can't donate tattered clothes, but still functional clothes or intact kitchen tools could be very useful to other people.

Part 2 Separate Objects Based on Room and Functionality

1

Separate objects based on their function. Examine them to decide how to divide them. Group similar items together to find the best way to store them. Maybe you can stack them, or insert one inside the other. If some things don't have a particular function, you could give them to charity.

2

Separate the objects according to the zone and the room they belong to. After grouping them by function, separate them again to arrange them in the most suitable room. Although some items have similar functions, you may need to place them in different parts of the house.

For example, cooking utensils should stay in the kitchen, so you can easily use them when you need them. Things you don't use often, such as an ice cream maker or large serving trays, can be stored in less accessible places.

3

Find strategic accommodation for items that can perform more than one function. If you have several things that perform the same functions, store them in different areas if possible.

A practical example of this type of item are small towels, which may be needed in the bathroom and kitchen

Part 3 Use Archiving Methods

1

Find the right place for each item. Things left lying around make rooms appear cluttered and disorganized, so find accommodation for everything. It's worth walking into a room, grabbing whatever object is within reach and wondering if that's where it should be. If it is is out of place, find suitable accommodation.

It is advisable to find specific accommodation for objects such as keys, cell phones and wallets. For example, make it a habit to always deposit these items in the same spot at the entrance. This way, you will avoid littering them around the house and leaving them in unsuitable places.

2

Store things in a functional way. They should take up as little space as possible, but be within reach. By organizing items in this way, you will have more space available and the house will look less cluttered.

Store smaller items in metal boxes, perhaps those of mints, to avoid confusing and losing them. Use labels to distinguish the various boxes and place them all in the same drawer.

You can use slats in a kitchen drawer to divide the lids of vacuum containers and keep them in place.

Attach metal plates to the inside of the cupboard so that you can use that space to attach recipes with magnetic clips instead of using the refrigerator panel.

Arrange necklaces on a hanger, earrings in an ice cube tray, bags on hangers.

Those plastic compartments can be very useful for all the small items like watches, make-up tools, batteries or accessories of various kinds.

Organize long-life foods (such as sugar and flour) in metal containers or glass jars because they are easy to stack and take up less space. The same goes for spices, which you can arrange next to the refrigerator.

You can store laundry products in a filing cabinet; arrange the kitchen cleaning products in a shoe rack to hang on the cupboard door.

3

Create a filing system. If you have multiple copies of the same item or a series of similar items, you may want to devise an effective way to keep them and find them easily when needed. On top of that, they would take up less space and you would have a larger area to exploit.

Get a filing cabinet or boxes for folders and documents. They are indispensable for organizing this type of material that you absolutely must not lose, such as tax documents, birth certificates and other important documents that you may need to find quickly.

Create a system for clothes too. Come up with a way to organize both clothes and soiled items. The latter can be separated by color in different baskets. Instead, clean clothes should be hung neatly, or folded in drawers or laundry baskets. Take a cue from flyers - roll up your clothes as you arrange them in drawers or baskets to minimize creasing and maximize space.

4

Think of a way to take advantage of the wasted space. Often, unused areas are perfect corners to store and organize your stuff. Find a way to take advantage of the free spaces to optimize the organization of the house.

If there is some space between the refrigerator and the wall, you might want to put shelves to accommodate jars and cans.

In almost all corridors there is space to insert a shelf on which to place various objects.

The space under the bed can be used to hide boxes (or bags) containing off-season linen, coats and voluminous sweaters.

Think about vertical spaces too. This excellent solution is often overlooked. That empty space between hanging clothes and the bottom shelf in a closet can be filled with shelves or used to hang shoes, belts or ties with special holders.

Part 4 Develop Good Habits

1

Think about each new item you buy. To keep an organized home you need to cultivate good habits: for example, it is worthwhile evaluating every object we come into possession of. Don't stockpile a lot of things you don't need, or you'll end up having a messy house again. Find a place for each item you buy.

2

Put everything in its place. Get in the habit of tidying up after using something. Don't put off or find justifications, thinking that maybe someone else might need it. Simply put back everything you use. This is the best habit for keeping a tidy and clean home.

3

Get in the habit of giving something to charity. Prepare a bag or box in which to store the items you would like to donate, especially those you no longer use. It would be a good idea to put a couple of items in the donation box every time you buy or receive a new one.

Advice

If you plan to make your home more organized, start with the area you use most often: for example, if you are a student, tidy up the room where you study, or the kitchen.

Think about the actual need to store certain things: for example, CDs take up a lot of space, but now most people use only iPods, MP3s and computers to listen to music. Convert your CDs to another format.

Find ways to reuse items you have around the house. For example, do you own a candle holder, but don't use candles? Use it as a pencil holder.

Americans are avid supporters of organization, so it is possible to find on the market many useful elements for organization of the house, without sacrificing style and fashion. This way, you no longer have to worry about hiding items you don't use often, because you can keep them in plain sight!

To keep the house organized, keeping the less used items, it is advisable to invest in the purchase of CD racks, bookcases and containers to put under the bed. If Christmas or your birthday is approaching, ask your relatives to give you some gift certificates to spend at Ikea, in furniture and DIY stores.

Warning

When organizing your home, minimize the risk of fire: for example, do not overload wall sockets with extension cords, do not store huge piles of newspapers and always leave the path to the exit free, because shoes and other items could get in the way of your escape in an emergency.

Be careful when moving furniture. Do not lift weights with your back, but with your legs. If possible, ask a friend for help.

CHAPTER 17 MISTAKES TO AVOID

Control freaks or chronically disordered? Clutter is not simply about visual chaos; it is the inability to find what we need when we need it. This is usually the case with messy people: they rush out in search of an object convulsively, exploring overflowing bags or closets where clothes have been thrown in bulk, creating even more chaos. If you want to become a more orderly person, focus on organization. What surrounds you must be easily found when you need it, this will save you time and stress in unnecessary searches. True order is a matter of mind, that's why.

Fast cleaning? Start dedicating 30 minutes every day to tidying up: the house reflects our state of mind, which is why it is important to take care of the environment in which we live and improve the quality of our life through the choices made every day.

Strategies for ordering the house

Piling creates chaos

Throwing away items in bulk does not help improve organization. Start cultivating a mental attitude to order: choose where to place each object in the house. An extremely functional way is to try to think by type of use. Instead of putting the objects where there is room or where they "fit", create a specific order so that you always know how to find what you need. For example, the jackets and accessories you use the most will be ready to wear in a place near the entrance. The books still to be read in a special shelf, while the reading of the moment in the magazine rack. Bills and deadlines? In plain sight, hung on a blackboard in the kitchen or a panel with post it notes and pins. Reasoning by categories of belonging and dividing the objects is the first step to clarify even on a mental level and gain time for the order of the house.

Getting used to tidying up

Bad habits increase disorder

When you come home at the end of the day, empty your pockets and throw away what you don't need. Are you standing in line in a waiting room and don't know how to use the time? Tidy up your bag! If you usually keep your receipts, put them all together in a diary or box. Preventing clutter will save you valuable time and never make you feel overwhelmed by chaos. To optimize house cleaning, avoid the classic drawer where you end up putting what does not have a place: not knowing what it contains is almost always useless! No more dishes and empty pockets where unnecessary objects risk accumulating. Avoiding clutter will help you be less chaotic.

Living in chaos makes your mood worse.

Books like The Magical Power of Tidying Up and the Konmari Method teach that living in chaos often has a negative influence on our mental state as well. Conversely, lightening the environment and making the home more essential can also improve our well-being. Look at your home. If there are boxes full of clothes and objects around and you don't know where to put them ... it's time to renew! Today we fight against the lack of space and often live in small houses, so it is important to make peace with this aspect by learning to live with the possibilities offered by space. In the kitchen, everything must be inside the cabinets: except for appliances such as toasters and knife holders, it is a strategy to eliminate the tendency to leave objects scattered on the table and gain an uncluttered work surface. Is there no place in the closet for all the clothes? You can add a box on the wardrobe or under the bed - as for the rest, make a choice! Learning to part from objects can be difficult at first, but it makes us lighter. Chaos clutters the mind.

Tidy wardrobe

Big spaces ... big mess!

Drawers that are too large and cabinets without dividers often increase the tendency for chaos. Splitting the space into smaller portions will help you manage your things better. In the closet, add some baskets or boxes that can hold smaller items, such as belts, briefs, socks, accessories. Avoid batteries! Better to fold T-shirts and sweaters in the drawers or hang the clothes most used in a certain period with a hanger. Decluttering will allow you to have a clear home and a better organized closet. We live in a consumerist society where there is a tendency to accumulate an excessive number of objects, ending up remaining slaves to the superfluous: living in the essential not only saves you time and money, but will benefit the quality of your life. Start with the overflowing drawer or the desk covered with documents, remove the dust, eliminate, position according to the category to which it belongs and have a bag ready to throw away everything you no longer need. Your home will have a new order and your mind will acquire lightness, good humor, inspiration.

CHAPTER 18 LEARN GOOD HABITS

When there are children in the family, keeping everything neat and tidy seems like a real dream. As babies they require care and attention, when they grow up they invade spaces with their toys. How then to face the daily routine without going crazy? Having a perfect home is not possible, but organizing yourself so as not to find yourself in chaos is. Here are some tips that require little daily effort but give maximum benefits, without forgetting that everyone must work together.

When the family grows, the house changes too. If before you could choose furniture in total freedom, now practicality and comfort must prevail in every aspect. Opt for welcoming but above all functional environments.

In the entrance, arrange child-height clothes hooks, in the bedroom put containers for books and toys, for the bathroom choose comfortable drawers with the necessaries for changing and bathing. Everything must have its place, so keeping things in order will be easier for everyone.

Order comes before cleaning

It is the first sore point when the family becomes larger: a quiet and orderly place becomes noisy and chaotic. Parents lose control of spaces that end up invaded by dolls and dinosaurs, socks, bottles and so on. If you let yourself go, confusion will reign. Start changing habits by memorizing a rule: a tidy room looks cleaner, even if there are two inches of dust on the shelves!

How to do it? Proceed with a new method: small daily tasks, less effort on the weekend.

Good habits of the day.

Establish some routine tasks. Every evening, before going to bed, pick up the misplaced things, arrange the laundry, load the dishwasher.

If you are an early riser, even better, take the opportunity to tidy up and clean quickly before waking the others.

Try not to go out without making the bed. Many debates the issue, but this simple gesture will help make your day more productive.

If you are a lover of lists, grab a pen and paper and list the things to do every day. But be careful not to become a slave to it, enter only what you can really do.

Adults and children, to each his own task.

Everyone must participate in the care of the house, starting with the older ones. It will also be a great example for your children. You can entrust them with simple tasks as early as two or three years old, to move on to more complex ones, such as drying the dishes, emptying the washing machine and, of course, putting the games back in their places.

Don't be too rigid, you have to make them understand the importance of mutual help by creating pleasant moments of sharing.

Always leave them the opportunity to do creative activities, such as tempera, paint, clay, but try to protect floors and surfaces. Again, the same principle applies: after playing, you clean up together.

Cleaning: better a little a day.

There are a number of basic operations when having children, also because, as everyone knows, their presence requires more attention to hygiene. Focus on the rooms that need special care: bathroom and kitchen. Clean the bathroom fixtures, wash the shelves, sweep the floor, do some quick dusting. Remember to peek under the sofa, you will discover an endless mine of marbles, dice and crayons.

If you can clean up a little bit of dirt every day, you won't end up with a mountain of backlog on the weekend. Also keep an eye on the laundry basket. With a load of washing machine every two days you will avoid being submerged by dirty clothes. Carefully follow the entire cycle: from washing the clothes until you hang them out. So you can iron better or even not iron at all!

Try not to accumulate.

Fewer things around, less effort. Make a selection from time to time of what is not needed, check the closets, drawers. It will be useful for you but also for your children. Getting them used to the idea of having less will help them understand the value of what they have and stimulate their creativity in playing games.

The decluttering can be fun if you do it all together: you have a series of different colored baskets to select the now broken objects (to fix or throw), those with whom you do not play more (to give away), the ones to keep.

Learn not to postpone.

The drops of juice on the floor, the crumbs from the snack, the paint on the table: you really never stop cleaning! Any stain, however, must be removed immediately, without postponing. Don't let yourself be lazy; take the cloth and wash it. It will be much easier to do it at that moment than to return when the dirt is difficult to remove.

Aim for a peaceful home, not a perfect one.

Clean yes, perfect no. As the family grows, you need to be less demanding. Especially if your children are still small, it is almost impossible for everything to work out perfectly. Better to take note of this and take on a new mentality: do not go crazy behind the frenzied rhythms of order and cleaning but try to create an atmosphere of serenity.

If you really can't do it, you can always ask for help but above all you have to learn to accept this phase of your life, and of your home, despite being full of defects.

And now, it's your turn: how do you manage to keep the clutter in the house under control? Do your children contribute to the housework? Share experiences and advice in the Comments.

CHAPTER 19 THE DECALOGUE FOR THE ORGANIZATION

Is it really possible to be organized even if you are not born with this ability, to be able to do everything effortlessly and save time? I'll reveal the 10 habits to adopt to be organized and productive!

Today I want to talk to you about the most effective habits to adopt to be more organized and productive since it is not necessary that you are an organized person from birth. Organization is something that can be learned and everyone can therefore become organized people, by simplifying their own life and reducing stress levels, yes everyone... even you! And at the end, you will have the clearest ideas on how to do it as well as the possibility of receiving a gift!

So, let's go!

1. The first habit of being organized is to WRITE EVERYTHING DOWN! In fact, relying on one's memory is really dangerous because there are so many things, life is unpredictable and it can happen that something escapes us, bringing with it the relative discomforts and a lot of stress in having to fix it.

You forgot to pay that bill and now you have a fine, you forgot to stop and buy that ingredient and now you can't prepare the dinner you planned, you forgot an appointment and maybe missed a great opportunity, you forgot to start the washing machine and now you don't have your uniform ready for work ...

Every time we forget something we should have done, we will inevitably have more or less negative consequences, we will find ourselves in difficulty, we will have to run ... why all this when you just have to write it down? You can keep a notebook with you in which you mark things on the fly or even just the notes of your cell phone.

Always mark everything: important dates, appointments, events, reminders, chores and you will discharge your mind of a great responsibility, feeling immediately lighter and less stressed. Yes, because when you keep everything in mind, you force your brain to continually think about what you have to do never allowing it to relax ... so if you want to avoid all this simply WRITE THINGS DOWN!

2.   The second habit that allows you to be more organized and above all more productive is NOT PROCRASTINATE or do not postpone things to do. In fact, many times we tend to postpone all those activities that weigh on us, that we do not like to do, perhaps using the excuse of being too busy and therefore of not having time to do them.

In fact, the procrastinator is generally a very busy person since he invents things to do in order not to do what really should be done. Very often, among other things, he postpones important things, activating also in this case negative consequences that could easily be avoided. To combat the tendency to procrastinate, you need to set specific goals with a deadline and simply START doing what you should!

Yes, because the hardest part is always getting started but once you have used your self-discipline to get started ... everything else will be downhill! And if the goal seems too big and discourages you ... divide it into small sub-goals also with precise deadlines. In fact, when the tasks are smaller it is easier to find the strength to start.

3. The third habit of organized people is to HAVE A PLACE FOR EVERYTHING AND EVERYTHING IN ITS PLACE, or to make sure that every object you have has its exact location so that you always know where to find it when you need it and where to put it back when it is no longer used. In fact, the organized person lives in organized environments that allow them to save time on a daily basis. It is therefore inevitable if you

want to start being more organized, look around and see the conditions of your home and, if necessary, start with improving this aspect.

4.   Relating to the previous point, the fourth habit of the organized person is TO AVOID ACCUMULATING DISORDER. In fact, when you tidy up what you use or in any case by the end of the day, the work to be done is very limited and can be completed in a few minutes, while if you let the mess accumulate, you will need much more time to tidy up and maybe, always having little time, you will have the tendency to postpone this task more and more until the situation becomes unmanageable.

Do not let an activity that can be solved really in a very short time, giving you the opportunity to always be organized and productive, turn into a mega work of hours and hours that maybe drags on up to lead you to negative consequences including that of living in an unwelcoming and uncomfortable environment.

5. Staying on the same theme, the fifth habit is ELIMINATING WHAT YOU DON'T NEED. It is not necessary for a person to marry the minimalist lifestyle to start decluttering, since relieving our homes of what we do not use, what is broken or that we keep for who knows what event that may never come, is something that benefits noone.

Our home must be pleasant to live in and functional to allow us to be organized and therefore why keep things that are not needed, clutter and only steal space and time uselessly? I will not add more on this point as I have talked about it extensively in all my videos on minimalism but it was essential to add it here as well as it is something extremely useful for those who want to improve their organization.

6. As for point number 5, the sixth habit of the organized person is TO BUY ONLY THE NECESSARY for several reasons: first of all, to avoid spending too much time on objects, then to keep everything in order

more easily and finally to have a better management of the own money by allocating it to things that really matter.

For this reason, a good suggestion is not to give in to the temptation of SALES ... always ask yourself if you really need that thing because even if it is taken for granted, if it is useless for you, you will still have wasted your money and once brought home you will waste your space and your time managing it. So, think carefully before making any purchases!

7. The seventh good habit of the organized person is to WAKE UP EARLY to have more time to do things ... many people complain of never having time and not being able to organize themselves always doing everything in bulk and in a hurry and then maybe if ask them what time they get up and they tell you 10 minutes before leaving the house.

It is normal that when you only have 10 minutes to prepare yourself and maybe even have breakfast, you cannot devote time to anything else and in addition, you risk arriving late and forgetting things, many small gestures that instead would allow you to make things work better.

Small actions of a few minutes that would greatly improve your day by saving you time... So why not wake up a little earlier to manage everything calmly?

8. The eighth habit is IMPROVING THE CONCENTRATION... the organized person in fact tends to fit all the activities in the best possible way and in order to carry them out in the shortest possible time he needs to keep his concentration high. There are several ways to train concentration... those that I recommend are Mindfulness meditation practiced both formally and informally during the day, and Yoga.

9. The ninth good habit of the organized person is NOT TO LEAVE THINGS HALF DONE. Each time you will have to make the effort to start over, perhaps fighting against the temptation to procrastinate ... Finally,

your brain will continue to think about it until you have completed it and this will increase your stress levels or your frustration.

10. Finally, the last good habit of the organized person is to create habits or a sequence of actions that are repeated day after day. The advantage of the routines is that first of all after a few days of repeating them, the brain will carry them out on automatic pilot almost completely eliminating the effort of doing them, furthermore, you will minimize the time needed to carry them out and you will not risk forgetting anything.

It is not necessary to have a life full of routine ... you just need a really efficient one to carry out every day to improve your organization and productivity significantly.

Well, these are the things that you should implement in your life if you want to become a more organized, I suggest you do not introduce them all at once. Start gradually by inserting a few at a time and only when they have been assimilated proceed with the others.

REMEMBER YOU HAVE TO TAKE ONE STEP AT A TIME.

CHAPTER 20 WEEKLY PLANNING

We are always in a hurry and busy, the frenetic pace of life leaves us little time at the end of the day to manage the house, yet we women of today still have to manage and always do some work at home.

When I got married and found my own home to take care of, I wasn't as organized as I am now. I perfected my method over time, between experience, comparisons with friends in the same situation and various internet searches.

The bulk of the housework is always done on Saturdays when, at home from work, I am able to dedicate myself completely to my sweet home. I want it to be as tidy and clean as possible, without expecting perfection every day. It's impossible!

During the week, I always took care of the little things like using the vacuum cleaner, keeping the bedroom, bathroom and kitchen tidy.

Because I decided to draw up the housework schedule.

All worked well for quite some time until new conditions came in: two children.

Needless to say, everything changed with the arrival of the children and nothing was ever the same again.

Children require time, care, attention, there are many more things to follow and the Holy Saturday morning of before has disappeared.

Result?

Chaos! Which has decided to move to my house, albeit without my consent.

We know that when children arrive, houses change their appearance, they adapt, they are not perfect, let's say that they are re- furnished in a fun, all-to-hand style, but the cleaning of the home environments must continue, and it is essential.

I spent a first period of a few weeks without knowing which way to turn, where to start, where to continue and if I would ever reach the end. I realized that I was jumping like a top from one room to another without getting anything done.

This was on a Saturday, the day I would have to sort out most of the things.

I let you imagine what I was able to accomplish every single day ... Suffice it to say that there were days when my husband and I had dinner two hours apart to be with the children and that I didn't even have the time to vacuum the crumbs off the kitchen tablecloth.

Fortunately, this is not normal and everything can be adjusted with a minimum of organization. From here, I decided to draw up a housework schedule, a plan for when to do the housework.

Why? To be organized, to optimize time by already knowing what I have to do and how much more or less time it takes me to complete what I have to do.

How? The goal was to be able to do some housework during the week, so that I can lighten up the Saturday so I can spend more time with the kids and with my husband.

How I planned the housework.

First of all, I made a list of things to do at home, dividing them into daily, weekly, monthly and yearly.

It is essential to know how much time you have available for home care every day and how long each single item on the list takes to be completed. Only in this way can we associate the work to be carried out by evening to days.

On this basis I compiled my planning.

You can see my schedule in the photos above. I have marked it both on the notice board of the Command Station at home and on my Notebook of Lists (which I will soon tell you about), an insert from my bullet journal.

Organizing house cleaning is not easy, especially for women who have to manage a family, home and work. With this weekly planner you can plan the daily household chores for the whole week and also write down the annual and monthly cleaning.

Useful for creating a daily cleaning routine, not to forget the areas of the house, which need more attention and care.

I made this cleaning planner to better manage the time available, to organize and clean the house and to also carve out some time for myself.

How to plan weekly house cleaning

To plan your house cleaning, you need to be aware of what you want to see cleaned each week and how much time you can spend on the house. Write your to-do list on a piece of paper as you look one room at a time.

At this point, according to the time you have available, divide the cleaning you will need to do to keep what you want clean. If necessary, write the same task several times throughout the week, such as dusting or cleaning the bathroom.

Keep in mind not to write too many chores in one day, so as not to overload yourself and risk not making it. There is always time to increase them if you are faster than expected.

Some weekly cleaning:

- dusting;
- cleaning the bathroom;
- cleaning the floors;
- cleaning the kitchen,

- vacuum;
- change the sheets;
- laundry;
- ironing.

House cleaning, monthly and yearly.

As for the monthly and annual cleaning, less frequent than the weekly ones and more difficult to remember, you can organize them in the same way, listing in the appropriate sections what you want to clean less frequently.

Don't forget to maintain your appliances to keep them efficient.

Some monthly and annual cleaning:

- remove cobwebs;
- seasonal cleaning: cleaning the interior and exterior of furniture, ornaments, curtains, chandeliers and everything else you need;
- change of season of wardrobes;
- cleaning of doors and windows;
- cleaning of window frames, windowsills and mosquito nets;
- cleaning of balconies or porches.

Tips for planning house cleaning and living peacefully.

One of the tips I feel like giving you is to live in the house without being a slave to it. Yes, I know, it is the classic phrase we hear but, I too was able to find a balance after years of endless cleaning.

Try to find a compromise, the house must be cleaned as necessary without stressing ourselves too much. Don't worry if your children leave their fingerprints again after cleaning the windows. I know, you would like to go and clean them immediately but, you enter a vicious circle and

you will go on forever, increasing the stress. You will clean them the next time they appear on your weekly schedule.

CHAPTER 21 THE PRINCIPLES OF MINIMALISM

The key principles of minimalism are essentially three: concentration on what is essential, removal of the superfluous and the pursuit of maximum enjoyment. Applying these principles in our life can be done in several ways, and in this chapter, I have collected some ideas to learn how to to let go of the things that do not add value to our life, to create space for us and to persevere in our principles even when it seems to us that it is impossible.

1. Focus on the whys

Living intentionally is essentially reconnecting to our whys. Asking why we do, buy, live, is the only way to discern between what is aligned with our life and what is not. And, it goes without saying, what is not aligned must not be part of it. Whenever you are called to make a decision, every time you are about to buy something, try to ask yourself why?

2. In case that... means never.

Every time we buy something or dedicate ourselves to an activity... We are just looking for an excuse to listen to the voice of the child inside us who wants to do what he likes, without listening to the adult who in our head explains that it would be useless. Every now and then it is good to listen to the child, and to dedicate ourselves to something that with the adult's hindsight we would not do, but even in these cases it is good to recognize that we are doing it because it is something that makes us feel alive. And since the world needs living people, we do it for this, ok? Does it seem inconsistent? That's life!

3. The 20/20 rule

All those times you find yourself about to buy something or say yes to an initiative, try to apply this rule coined by Joshua Fields Millburn and Ryan Nicodemus. If it takes you less than twenty minutes and less than twenty dollars to buy that thing when you need it, forget it for now.

Personally, I twisted this rule to make it valid beyond physical things as well. If something takes me less than twenty minutes and costs less than twenty dollarss, I'll let it go. Sure, then there are exceptions, but basically things of little value that require little effort are distractions.

4. One thing at a time

More than a rule for being minimalist, this is a principle of productivity good for any occasion, and fundamental for those who want to live minimally. When we are totally focused on one thing, one thing only, it is less difficult to eliminate the distractions, the superfluous, everything that does not have to do with our whys. This is why I often write with headphones on, or in conditions of total solitude. If we strive every week to eliminate a distraction, within a year we will have eliminated from our life over 50 factors that prevent us from living it to the full.

5. Take it easy

Think of quality not quantity .. It is not important to do everything in life, but to do what we do well, otherwise we will end up doing a lot of bad things, with the only result of not having done anything. If everything matters, nothing really matters. Furthermore, the only thing that matters is to progress, to advance towards the realization of one's goals. Celebrating small wins is the only way to recognize that we are progressing towards success.

6. Look at yourself

There is always someone with a more beautiful car, the latest iPhone, a more expensive dress or who simply goes on vacation to exotic countries that we have only seen in travel agency brochures. So? He may be less happy than you. As researcher Shawn Achor discovered when studying the relationship between happiness and success, there are happy people even in conditions that seem dramatic to us. If we look at what remains after we have removed what does not give us a reason, we are left alone with what gives us pleasure and is part of us. Could you be happier?

7. Minimalism is not....

Being minimalist does not mean eliminating everything we have, but keeping only what really gives us pleasure. A minimalist wardrobe is not based on fewer items than a normal one (even if it is), but on the 20 percent of items we wear because they really give us pleasure. By applying the Pareto principle to our wardrobe, in fact, we could in fact eliminate 80 percent of clothes because we wear them once in a while, often just because we own them, and that if we had to buy them back today, we would not spend a single dollar. This rule can be applied in every area of life, from the apps you have on your phone to the people you hang out with.

8. It costs more to keep things than to give them away

Make two accounts: every object costs you time and energy. Think about the entrance hall of your home: if there was only one photo, for example that of your wedding, or your family, every day you would be greeted by the memory of a happy moment. Instead, cramming that wall with pictures, each one of them requires some time of your attention and it ends up that none of them ever get it.

9. Evaluate spaces

We live in two spaces that are not very different from each other: one real, and one mental. In the first, the only way to generate value is to start from a careful observation of the (physical) spaces required by each object that surrounds us, as well as the empty (physical) spaces we need to move and enjoy what we have. The more space there is, the more time we have to enjoy what is in this space. Likewise, the more space we have in our mind the more clarity we can have about our thoughts and actions, and this is one of the main reasons I decided to start meditating and continue to do so.

10. Decluttering in every area

Remember with fewer items on your bedside table you sleep better. So get rid of the superfluous in any room.

11. Quality vs quantity

The best rule to follow for a truly minimalist life is only quality things. An 80 dollars pair of pants, apart from the brand, is definitely better than a 20 dollars pair. To afford them we have to give up three extra pairs of trousers, but as Pareto teaches us, even if we had them we would probably give up because of the four we would wear one more often and the others every now and then. Isn't it better then to give up those three and take the best one directly? Which, moreover, will most likely last longer over time, and therefore will allow us to save something in the long run.

Imagine if you only had five or six pairs of pants that you like a lot instead of having a dozen that you never wear many of - wouldn't that be nice? Before you spend your money on something new, ask yourself if this is the best you can get. If it's not, save your money for when you find what's worth spending it on. And when you find it, don't mind the expense!

12. Don't feel guilty

Throw away anything you don't like, even if someone you are/were romantically attached to gave it to you. Those who love you want you to live well, not overwhelmed with junk that you keep just so as not to feel guilty, so if you keep something you don't like you cause them real sorrow. Furthermore, surrounding yourself with objects, or experiences, of others - or that you have bought in case imprisons you in the life that others have imagined for you, moving away from the one you want to live!

13. The 90/90 rule

Another rule initiated by Joshua Fields Millburn and Ryan Nicodemus. If you haven't used something in the past three months, pick it up and ask yourself if you would use it in the next three. If the answer is no - net of seasonality - donate it to someone else or throw it away.

14. Be grateful for what you have

Gratitude is not only a consequence of minimalism, but also a way to get there. Keeping a gratitude journal helps us to take time each day to enjoy the pleasant times we have lived, to find something worth living for.

+1. Learn the rules so you can break them!

As in everything, to become an expert you need to learn and practice the rules. It is only when we have made them our own, however, that we can create our variants to make them suitable for our life, and why not, improve them.

CHAPTER 22 HOW TO ORGANIZE THE CLOSET

A well-organized closet is the first step in keeping a room and your life tidy. Go through your entire wardrobe to decide which items you really need, then you have to find the best way to rearrange everything, clothes and everything in between.

Part 1 Examine the Wardrobe

1

Remove all the clothes from the closet. Take them out of drawers, containers and take out the hangers. Fold them and arrange them in neat piles on the floor or bed, along with all the shoes.

Expert Advice

"Tidy up your wardrobe as often as possible. The more frequently you clean it, the less effort you will need to do it".

2

Decide which clothes you want to keep. It's not worth throwing away the clothes you use regularly, the ones you would need if they weren't already in your wardrobe. If you wore a certain dress during the last week, last month, or a few months ago, don't delete it from your wardrobe, as long as it's suitable for the current season. Create a pile of clothes to keep - the ones you wear regularly.

3

Decide which clothes you will put aside. You need to keep items that you won't be wearing for a while because they aren't suitable for the current season. If it's midsummer, keep your winter sweaters and scarves; instead, if it's winter you should put away your summer tops and dresses.

When you're done selecting your clothes, put them in a plastic container to store in the closet, under the bed, in the garage, or elsewhere in the house.

Rearrange your closet seasonally.

4

Determine which items you can donate and which ones are to be thrown away.

If a garment is extremely frayed, moth-eaten and faded, no one will likely be able to wear it again, so throw it away.

If some clothes are too tight, don't wait until the day you start the diet, but donate it.

Donate any clothes in good condition that you don't need, or give them to a relative or friend.

5

Clean the inside of the closet. You must do this before putting the clothes back in place. Vacuum, remove dust, clean the walls with a cleaner and remove any cobwebs.

If you are planning to modify the wardrobe in any way, like painting it a different color, adding or removing shelves, now is the time to do it.

Part 2 Organize Clothes in the Closet

1

Hang your clothes in the closet and organize them. Hang all the clothes you can. You don't just have to hang them, but arrange them in a particular order that allows you to find them more easily. Here's how to do it:

Organize your clothes according to the season. Organize clothes according to the type of garment; for example, it groups all the tank tops, then the shirts, trousers, skirts and dresses.

Separate your work and leisure clothes.

Arrange your clothes according to how often you wear them. Choose the organization system you prefer, but hang the clothes you wear most often in the most accessible place.

You can use different color hangers.

Arrange them by color. For example, use pink for shirts, green for work clothes, and so on.

If there is room, you could add another rod to hang more clothes.

2

Arrange the other clothes in different places in the closet. After hanging the clothes, you use most on the rod, put the rest of the clothes in order. Place the ones you use less frequently and the items that don't need to hang in the plastic containers. Here are some ideas:

Don't waste space under hanging clothes. At that point you can arrange some container or a chest of drawers.

You could add elements to the closet to organize the various spaces more efficiently.

3

Organize your shoes. Arrange them according to the model in a shoe cabinet, which you could place at the entrance to the house. Taking off your shoes as soon as you enter the house is an excellent habit to keep the house clean.

Part 3 Organize the Rest of the Closet

1

Organize all the boxes. If the closet is spacious enough, you probably have not only kept your clothes inside, but also boxes full of souvenirs, photo albums and CDs that you haven't used in years. To complete the job, you should examine the contents of the boxes and select the items to keep, throwing the rest away. Here's how to do it:

Get rid of all magazines and items stored for years even if they have sentimental value.

Arrange the boxes and group them together to save space. If the closet is already full, you may want to store a few items in different places. For example, arrange photo albums on a shelf or in the bookcase.

If you have used cardboard boxes so far, replace them with plastic containers as they are stronger and more eye-catching.

Apply labels to containers and boxes to know what they contain. They will make your work easier the next time you tidy up the closet.

2

Organize whatever is left.

If you left a box of light bulbs, comics or chocolates in the closet, it would be better to move them somewhere else, finding a location more suited to the type of object.

3

Make the closet eye-catching. You can really indulge yourself in adding a touch of style to the wardrobe, considering that you use it every day. If you embellish it in any way, in the future you will think twice before leaving everything in a mess.

Paint the doors with a nice pastel color;

Add some mirrors to make it brighter;

Hang jewelry and scarves in plain sight, as long as they are not in the way;

Hang a small poster or painting inside that will put you in a good mood when you see it.

Advice

Metal hangers aren't the best. Use plastic, wooden, or fabric-covered models as they rarely cause problems or stain clothing.

Shoe racks that attach to the doors are great for saving space compared to normal models that rest on the ground.

If there is enough floor space in the closet, you could also add a chest of drawers.

The plastic crates used for transporting milk are perfect for organizing the cupboard. You can stack them and arrange sweaters, sweatshirts, shoes and much more.

CHAPTER 23 HOW TO ORGANIZE THE DRAWERS OF THE DRESSER

When you open the dresser, do you think you see a curled-up raccoon inside? Do you feel like you have more clothes than you can keep? The solution to these problems is to rearrange your drawers: in this way, you can wear all your favorite clothes, instead of always wearing the usual two or three T-shirts.

Part 1 Select Clothes

1

Choose the items to get rid of. Start the "drawer organization" operation by removing everything you see inside. Examine each outfit and decide which ones to remove. Look for the ones that don't fit you, the old-fashioned ones, the ones that are stained or worn, and the ones you don't wear very often. You can give away clothes that are in good condition, but those that are in bad condition should just be thrown away. Even if they have long gone out of fashion, you may want to keep some, perhaps because they have sentimental value. Try to find another intended use, such as making a rug or t-shirt blanket, so they won't take up space in your drawers.

If it's a casual or everyday garment and you haven't worn it for a year, now is the time to get it out of the way. Dresses for formal occasions can last a little longer, even if they are not worn often.

2

Separate them according to the season. Once you know which ones to keep, sort your clothes according to the time of year. You can make the change of seasons by storing the less appropriate ones in a plastic container stored in the closet or basement, until they are needed again.

You can also store off-season items by placing them in boxes to put under the bed.

At the very least, try storing heavier winter clothes in the lower drawers. It will also be better for your chest of drawers.

3

Organize clothes by gender. Organize all the clothes according to their type. Normally, you can classify them into delicates, pajamas, casual and elegant shirts, casual and elegant trousers, heavy and light sweaters. Trousers should be stored separately, like sweaters, so try to set aside a drawer for these items only.

Typically, these items can be easily divided between four drawers. Delicates and pajamas in one, shirts in the second, trousers in the third and sweaters and other items in the fourth.

4

Organize clothes according to their usefulness. Within each category that you have established, it will be appropriate to arrange the garments according to how they should be stored within their section. You can divide them by utility or by color as you like.

If you want to follow the criterion of utility, separate them by looking at the similarities: light garments vs heavy garments, casual clothes vs elegant clothes, more provocative clothes vs work clothes, and so on. Keep together even those that have similar fabrics.

The color separation will give your drawers a much nicer look and help you find the right motivation to keep them organized.

5

Separate your clothes once you have established the best way to store them. Having all the clothes divided in front of you, you will have to decide which ones to store and in which drawers. In general, it is best to put the clothes you use most often on top.

Special care may be required for certain types of clothing. For example, to combat moths it is important to put a cedar tablet or mothballs in the drawers that contain the sweaters.

You may even need to hang certain clothes or arrange them in protective bags rather than drawers. Therefore, it would be better to keep silk or more expensive garments, separate them from others and especially the expensive sweaters, put in moth-proof bags.

Part 2 Divide the Clothes

1

Divide the drawers into sections. Usually, a drawer is too large to hold various types of clothing. So visually divide it into compartments. For longer drawer's three-part division will work, while for smaller ones two sections will suffice.

The compartments can be further divided according to need. For example, you could divide the longer upper drawer into three parts: in the first you can arrange the bras, overlapping them; in the second put socks and pajamas, separating them into two other compartments; the third can be divided into three other sections to be used for different types of underwear.

2

Try using containers. Use open containers, such as the wicker or fabric baskets you see in home improvement stores, to respect the divisions established in the drawers. Get containers of different sizes and put them in the drawers. You can arrange the clothes inside them.

3

Try using dividers. Get some similar to extendable curtain rods, but flatter, and adjust them to the size of the drawers. You can easily buy them at stores where household items are sold, such as baskets and ironing boards. You can make cardboard or foam dividers.

Or use those contained in packaging multiple of wine.

4

Try using bookends. Place them in drawers and you will get a simple but functional solution to divide the space inside.

However, they are perfect for sweaters, jeans and rolled-up sweaters.

Part 3 Store Clothes Functionally

1

Try rolling your clothes. You've probably heard of how practical rolled-up clothes are when packing your bags. The drawers at home make no difference. Rolled up, your garments will take up less space and avoid wrinkling if you do this correctly. Roll them slowly, with a certain symmetry and tightly, to prevent them from creasing.

2

Use a shirt-folding cardboard. When folding clothes, use a shirt-folding cardboard. It is a sheet or a piece of cardboard, similar to a clipboard, which is used during the phases of folding shirts and trousers. Place it in the center of the shirt near the collar. Place the left sleeve over the right, folding it along the side of the cardboard, and then repeat for the right sleeve. If necessary, adjust both sleeves and then fold the bottom edge of the shirt. For the pants, simply fold them in half and then wrap them around the cardboard.

It is a system that facilitates the organization of garments and their overlapping in a very similar way to that used to neatly display shirts on store shelves.

To make your shirt folder, cut a rather thick piece of cardboard measuring 38x45cm.

3

Place the items in a row, do not stack them. When storing clothes in drawers, do not stack them. This is the most common way to put clothing in a drawer, but it is very easy to crease and it is more difficult to find what you need. Instead of stacking them, "line them up". You can roll them up and place them perpendicularly or sideways, or fold them with a shirt folder and store them in a row.

4

Slip the bras into one another. For a space-saving solution, you can arrange them along a single large line or place the left cup inside the right, although this method risks deforming the central part of the bra.

Advice

Give away clothes if they are not damaged.

If you have enough space in the closet, hang larger and more voluminous items. Drawers are more functional for smaller and more numerous items.

Get rid of the clothes you don't like any more.

You can also not fold the underwear. Nobody will come to check if it's wrinkled and you will save time every time you have to fix the laundry.

CHAPTER 24 THE KONMARI METHOD

We all need more order in our lives. This is proved by the success of the KonMari method by Marie Kondo, which in a few years has conquered those who made disorder a lifestyle (or simply did not have time to tidy up).

What is usually missing is time, looking for ways to save it and doing things so that next time it is easier to tidy up the house or find kitchen utensils, is what the book focuses on: "The magical power of tidying", which now stands on the bedside tables of those who want to embrace this new method.

The philosophy behind it is to let go of all objects that do not make us happy or that do not give us positive feelings.

Basically, the rules are few and simple and are based on the concept of happiness and slowness, of relaxation and serenity. If we don't need a garment or it doesn't communicate anything to us, why keep it? And why take up more space by balling up clothes, when there is a more effective method of folding them?

In 2015 Marie Kondo was proclaimed one of the 100 most influential personalities according to Time and in 2019 Netflix dedicated a series to her. If you have been looking for a long time to put your house in order, but find it tiring, here are some ideas from the KonMari method.

Let's see these 10 rules together to become part of the magical world of tidying up:

1) Reorder for use

Proceeding by use: the order in which you store things will be the one in which you will use them, so think carefully about how you live in the spaces before proceeding with the cleaning! First throw away anything you don't use and anything that is visibly worn or deteriorated.

2) How to arrange bags

You will never believe it, but the best way to keep bags beautiful and tidy is to insert them one inside the other according to the shape according to Marie Kondo. The reason is simple: the larger ones will hold the medium ones and the medium ones will hold the small ones. Obviously, it is advisable to keep the shoulder straps in sight so as not to forget them between one season and another.

3) Keep the objects that stir up memories

If an object has an important history for you, it is right to keep it: an old cigarette lighter, a set of glasses, a vase, can arouse in us emotions, daily, as they are linked to particular moments of our life. So, keep these items for as long as you want.

4) Fold the clothes into origami

You don't need to know the fine Japanese art of origami to fold clothes to save space! In fact, Marie Kondo suggests forming a rectangle with the garment, folding it lengthwise in two and then folding it lengthwise in two or three. By storing it vertically in the closet or drawers, you will get much more space for the rest of the wardrobe.

5) A custom-made wardrobe

Not all wardrobes are the same and not all are suitable for our needs. The important thing is to visualize: make a drawing of the space you would need in the wardrobe and give it a shape; this will make it easier to choose the wardrobe that best suits you and your home. The element of personalization is important to keep the clothes you have decided to keep in order.

6) Hang the clothes in the wardrobe

There are those who hang them only by color and the result is certainly of impact, but according to the KonMari method it is better to hang the clothes and jackets also in order of fabric, or from the heaviest to the lightest. The longer, heavier and darker garments will go to the left to begin the roundup of hangers (if possible, get them all the same and thin) up to light and short clothes.

7) How to pack

Perhaps no one has ever thought of filling the suitcase vertically and not horizontally. In fact, the vertical side is longer and allows us to use more surface. Always fold the clothes so that they take up less space, the suits instead, which cannot be folded into origami, can be folded in two and arranged horizontally on the rest. Always choose to also reduce the volume of shampoos or creams by replacing the original jars with travel jars. Once the suitcase is unpacked, also clean it externally to store it until the next use.

8) Order in the home and in life

Creating order can make us tired, and if we proceed in stages the work will be longer. Instead, decide to gather everything to rearrange in a single point, proceeding one at a time to decide what you want to keep and what gives you an emotion, and what can be given away or thrown away. You will always find yourself in an impeccable home and retrace the important stages of your life at the same time.

9) Find a place for ourselves

"There is no place like home," said Judy Garland in the famous Wizard of Oz. And in fact, in which place, if not your home, is it more suitable to create a corner dedicated to us and our regeneration? A place to relax and recharge your batteries? The objects that will surround you in this space are also important, look for your favorites and furnish this little corner of paradise.

10) Proceed by categories

The most important rule, however, is never to lose focus. When we are surrounded by clutter we can be tempted to proceed by room, but in reality, the best thing is to put in place the second category: all the clothes, all the books, all the kitchen utensils and so on. In this world we will save time and group together all the similar objects that we happen to use every day.

 Getting rid of useless objects helps to make space not only in your home or office but also in your life because only by setting aside what is old can we really be able to welcome the new.

The Konmari method on the whole may seem quite drastic but if we do not want to apply it in its entirety there are no problems since we can still take a cue from Marie Kondo's advice simply to have a tidier wardrobe.

Both in Japan, where she was born, and all over the world, Marie Kondo is now considered an international expert in the art of tidying up. She is now very famous because of the books she has written and the television shows she has participated in.

Of course, embracing the Japanese mentality, which is really very minimalist, is not easy, but we can still draw some useful advice from the author's books.

Over the years we accumulate many objects and some of them, with the passage of time, we no longer need, yet we continue to keep them, perhaps because they are memories or even because we think they could be useful to us in the future.

The order of the physical space in which we live is reflected in order and a feeling of calm in our mind. This explains in a nutshell why living in an orderly space makes us feel more relaxed and organized.

Konmari method, how to tidy up the kitchen

According to the Konmari method, it is certainly not the dishes and glasses that we use every day but the kitchen utensils that take up a lot of space in our kitchens. Many utensils have really been lying in kitchen drawers for a long time, even though we haven't used them for years. At this point, if we really need to make space, we should make a selection of the utensils to keep at hand every day in the kitchen and those that we could store elsewhere because they are little used and take up precious space.

Konmari method, sheets and blankets

You should never leave sheets, pillowcases and blankets trapped in their plastic bags because unfortunately they tend to retain moisture. You risk finding moldy old sheets or pillowcases that may have remained in a very humid place. Better to keep only the pillowcases, sheets and blankets that our family and guests really need. To make room in the wardrobe we can give away sheets and blankets that we no longer need. The sheets and pillowcases that you usually use to change the bed should be kept within reach in the closet.

Konmari method, towels

You never know where to put the towels? Marie Kondo gives us a very logical answer in this regard. Towels should be placed in the most useful place where they should be, i.e. in a cabinet near the bathroom so that they are always available when it is time to use them. Even old towels that you would like to use as rags should never be rolled up but you should fold them just like the others so that they take up as little space as possible. Of course, you can separate old towels from new towels and guest towels.

Konmari method, sweaters

To fold sweaters, follow the basic method already indicated for the t-shirts and in addition add these instructions useful for both sweaters and all long-sleeved shirts, following the image.

Konmari method, hooded and high-necked sweaters

For hooded and high-necked sweaters, you must follow the same procedure valid for sweaters with the difference of having to fold the hood or the high collar down after folding the sleeves so that it is inside the garment to be stored in the wardrobe.

Konmari method, stockings and tights

According to the Konmari method, stockings should not be tucked into each other and rolled up while tights should not be knotted at all because they risk getting damaged. Both stockings and tights must be treated carefully and must always be folded lengthwise, trying to form rectangles or squares as for all other garments. Even in the drawers, socks and tights should be arranged vertically and not horizontally as we are used to. In this way we will not have to dig into the drawers to find the right socks because we will immediately recognize them from above by seeing the edge.

Konmari method, change of season

The Konmari method shows us how to avoid the change of season. Noting the change of season is necessary for those who have the habit of storing summer clothes that will not be needed during the winter season in boxes to be placed in the upper part of the wardrobe and vice versa. Marie Kondo, on the other hand, suggests you can overcome this type of obstacle, and to divide the clothes according to the material from the outset by providing, for example, very specific drawers for light cotton sweaters and other drawers for heavy or woollen sweaters without ever mixing the whole. So even in summer you will have some heavy clothes on hand in case the temperatures drop from time to time.

Konmari method, don't throw away, donate!

Often the author, in her books, suggests throwing away everything that is no longer needed literally and without remorse and on this point we do not feel at all in agreement. Fortunately, there are many alternatives to throwing clothes, books, accessories, utensils and objects of various kinds in the trash. In fact, you can give to those who need it or donate to charity what is no longer needed, or barter or resell it. There are now many channels, both online and at thrift shops and bartering outlets, which facilitate gifting, exchange and sale. It would really be a shame to allocate goods to the landfill that can still have great value and maximum usefulness for other people.

CHAPTER 25 TIPS FOR ORDERING THE LIVING ROOM

Although it is a multipurpose space, in which to spend especially the time of relaxation, the risk of accumulation and disorder is always present.

Keep only a selection of books on view: the ones you like best, those of art or simply those with the most beautiful covers.

This way you won't have to dust too many shelves and keep them tidy.

The other books (and CDs) can be hidden inside some cupboards, so that they are still within reach.

In general, use the open shelves to expose a few, selected objects. If you don't know how to choose, you could periodically rotate the exhibits, so as to change the setting, as if it were a small personal exhibition!

You can do the same thing with paintings, posters and prints, by rotating the hanging works like in a museum!

Use a chest or trunk to store the blankets, spare sofa cover and extra pillow cases. If there is space left, you can store other household linens that you don't use very often.

If you have a sideboard, use the space above it too, but without cramming in too many things: maybe you can arrange a nice decorated paper box and a hanging decorative plant.

Look around and study the possibilities: often in the living room it is possible to create some niche to be transformed into a built-in wardrobe.

Organize the cables of television, stereo, video game consoles, etc. with the appropriate tubes or with clamps that help to keep them in order: if your TV cabinet does not have it, consider whether it is convenient to make a circular hole on the back wall, to pass all the cables through (modern furniture usually already comes with them).

For the sofa area, choose a coffee table that has a lower shelf, so you can arrange the magazines and perhaps the basket with your latest knitting.

Alternatively, or in addition, you can use one of those hanging pockets on the side of the sofa (where it is less visible) to store the remote control and the book you are reading.

If your apartment opens up directly onto the living room, even plan a console with some nice bowls, if necessary, hold the objects in order, but when they are empty will decorate the environment.

CHAPTER 26 HOW TO ORGANIZE A SMALL BATHROOM

Putting on make-up and taking care of our beauty routine is a treat, relaxes us and cheers us up. It can be frustrating to do it in an environment that is not functional or that we do not feel is "ours". Often on social media we see celebrities wearing make-up in huge and luxurious bathrooms, but even a small bathroom can become delightful, and perfectly suited to our needs. We then decided to collect a few ideas to transform our small bathroom into a warm and comfortable space, even spending very little.

THINKING VERTICALLY

Having little "usable surface" available, we take advantage of verticality! But given that the space is already small, this does not mean hanging a thousand shelves full of objects on the walls.

A good idea is to hang towels, strictly clear, a bit like in hotels. There is nothing like soft colors, such as white, beige or powder pink, to optically enlarge the space by creating a bright and uncluttered environment.

On the other hand, it must be said that many cosmetics are also beautiful objects to look at. So, two or three small shelves on the sides of the mirror are welcome, containing the products we use every day and that in this way will always be on hand ... even when we are rushing!

Always "thinking vertically", a space to be absolutely exploited is that, partially hidden, next to the sink. Here you can hang a container intended for a hairdryer, which will always be convenient to reach even when it comes to taming a single rebellious tuft that has sprung up or treacherously during the night.

Above the door is another great area to place a shelf with various products. It's another idea to make the space appear larger and make the overall effect cleaner and tidier.

CHAPTER 27 CONCLUSIONS

For sure you have always noticed this, but you may not have known that there is scientific evidence to confirm it: mental health and a clean and tidy home have many points in common. It's something we've been hearing a lot about lately, so much so that decluttering - the activity of throwing away everything we no longer need - has become a very popular activity. In fact, experts in the sector and everyone agrees that a crowded house is also a sign of a crowded mind, and that to live better you need to get rid of useless objects.

Not only decluttering, however, serves to keep the mind in the right conditions of balance, but all activities related to the cleaning and order of one's home. Are you curious to know why and how to make your home a place where the mind can rest and regenerate? Then you just have to keep reading!

Relieve stress with intensive cleaning.

It's a benefit that people who tend to get angry often know very well: nothing helps relieve stress more than rubbing the tiles until they are shiny like a mirror. In fact, cleaning is sometimes a tiring activity, which certainly requires a lot of energy and concentration. The extra advice? Find out which is the best steam cleaner on the market: nothing is better for relieving stress than knowing that you have killed all the germs and bacteria.

Meditate while sanitizing the house.

Household cleaning is an excellent adjunct to meditation. Don't believe it? So, think: for the house to be really clean, you have to focus on repeating a series of actions in a specific order. Now it's clearer, huh? Concentrating only on cleaning, and while you clean, focusing only on the object you are healing at the moment will eliminate any unnecessary thoughts from your mind. After cleaning, your mind will also be cleaner and you will feel more at peace.

Increase productivity by learning to optimize.

By cleaning your home, you learn how to become a better professional. How? Learning to program, optimize times, get better and better results in less time. A fully-fledged mental training, which can also become your routine at work, making you much more productive people.

Mens sana in corpore sano

A clean, neatly organized home immediately gives a feeling of both physical and mental well-being. In fact, after passing the steam cleaner over the mattress and all the textiles, you can breathe and sleep better, and this is a great help to start the day more rested.

Living in a tidy home helps you feel more at peace.

Even though lazier people seemingly feel at peace by putting off cleaning in favor of a nice nap, actually living in clutter is extremely tiring. Not only because it usually takes twice as long to find anything, but also because the disorder creates over-stimulation for the eyes and brain. Conversely, ordering helps save time, and returns a soothing image that instantly calms the nerves.

Order and cleanliness reduce domestic conflict and help sociability.

The habit of systematically leaving one or more areas of the house dirty or in disorder is, as we know, one of the first sources of domestic conflict. And, you can't live well, in peace and without stress, in a house where you spend time arguing. Furthermore, people who have always dirty and untidy homes tend to reduce their sociability, because they are ashamed of the judgment of others.

The result is fewer friendships and moments of leisure, and more discussions and jitters. Not quite ideal for feeling good. Advice? Develop the art of delegation, empower everyone and assum the leadership of the house. It is also used to educate children to take care of their belongings, as well as to make the house a welcoming environment in which to feel good.

By adopting some simple daily habits of order and cleaning, keeping the house tidy becomes simple.

The health benefits are at least three:

Lower risk of disease. Accumulation of dust and bacteria is a common cause of allergies and other reactions.

Good mood. Who doesn't like seeing order and smelling a pleasant smell in the house?

Exercise. Cleaning involves an energy expenditure which, however moderate, is good for the body. Eventually, you will feel satisfied and relieved.

How to get into the habit of maintaining order in the house? With a few simple gestures. You will see, it is small daily efforts that make life easier.

If you set aside five minutes a day to clean the floor, you will find that keeping it clean will be easier. Do not allow dust or food spillages to accumulate: sometimes it is sufficient to pass the broom or a damp cloth. Try to do this every day after eating.

2. Make the beds to keep the house tidy

Yes, we know it's one of the most annoying jobs. Making the bed, stretching the sheets, but it gives the bedroom an immediate sense of order. Do it in the morning, before you go out. If you can, leave the windows open to ventilate. Wash the sheets weekly with hot water.

3. Fold clothes or put them on hangers

Clothes scattered everywhere are one of the elements that contribute to making the appearance of a house less pleasant.

As soon as you get back into the house, hang up your jacket. After taking a shower, put your dirty clothes in the basket. Place your clothes for the next day folded on a chair, or in their place in the closet. These are small gestures with an enormous visual impact.

4. Clean the shower and bathroom every day

It may seem tedious to clean the shower after using it, but it's a great habit. You can wipe the walls with a cloth with disinfectant liquid to prevent soap or mold residue from accumulating. Take a couple of minutes to clean the toilet and sink as well. The appearance of the bathroom will change dramatically.

5. Establish a time for collective cleaning every day

To keep the house tidy while engaging the whole family, try assigning a task to each member: washing the dishes, taking out the trash, feeding the dog, or sweeping the floors.

These are small tasks that, if left unresolved, together increase the sense of guilt and heaviness. Sharing tasks helps develop a sense of responsibility in children and improves coexistence at home.

Last, but not least: the above does not mean that you have to "live to clean". There is no need to go to extremes to maintain your well-being and balance.

Rather, it is about finding a routine that helps us to live in a healthy and pleasant environment, without obsession but with constancy.

The liveability of any home, starting from the smallest studio apartments, certainly grows with order. Knowing how to organize the interior spaces of our home can help us a lot in this, also because, you know, we are all a bit lazy when it comes to ordering. Often, however, tidying up the house from head to toe is not easy and we can think that we do not know where to start. For a sure result, here are *9 simple and achievable tips for ordering any environment and even your mother will be amazed by the order that reigns in the house (or in your bedroom).*

1. Identify the areas of the house that are most used. We could divide the zones of each environment into active, meaning those places of the house used daily, where we spend every day or where we spend part of our time. And, of course, passive, that is, those corners where you never stop, you don't pass and often don't even look. Ideally divided the house into active and passive areas, we can "fill" them by differentiating objects of daily use and objects of sporadic or no use. The former will be placed in convenient places to reach; the latter, on the other hand, can be stored in the less used areas of the house. In this case, we are also talking about the most uncomfortable drawers or shelves to reach or about unused corners in everyday life such as the basement, for example, or the space created between the wall and a wardrobe.

2. Value the so-called open solutions. These are those places where you store objects and knick-knacks that are visible, therefore shelves and shelves, tables and display cabinets, whose fillings are always under the eye of those who live in that environment. And which therefore should be enhanced with objects or a set of objects pleasing to the eye, colored or valuable. Probably no one would ever have spare bulbs on the shelves in the living room, party games with old and worn boxes or garden tools... And there is a reason! Preferably you can use, just a classic example, books for the living room, crystal sets for the kitchen or for the display cabinets.

3. Simplicity is the golden rule. To increase the ease of finding objects, it is useful to arrange the most used ones in easy-to-reach places, so that it is also more instinctive to store them in order after their use. If I put the stationery items in the study in a box, in a cupboard, on a high shelf, they are more likely to remain on the desk than to return to their place.

4. Give priority to availability. To find everyday objects with ease, it is advisable to store them in places that are easy to reach and use. In the kitchen, for example, we can order transparent jars for utility or alternatively label them with the name of the content (or maybe a photo?). In the bedroom, however, especially in the children's room, we use open baskets, so that it is possible to know their contents at a glance.

5. Group objects by categories. When ordering your things, it is always useful to group everything you may need for a particular job in the same place, as is done, for example, with the toolbox. To do this, cabinet boxes or even usable independent boxes come to the rescue. The most classic example is that of the medicine box or office supplies. It is important to always use labels that say what the contents of the particular box are, so that it is intuitive to find what we need and also put it back in its place.

6. Create a safe passageway. That is, find a space near which you need to pass before leaving the house. A place where passing objects can be temporarily left, such as those on loan or those that need to be repaired. But above all, where you can store the essential items when you go out, such as house keys, car keys, wallet. In order to have a place to store them once you return and where you are sure to always find them, especially when we are clearly late.

7. Learn how to use drawers. Drawers and chests of drawers are the realm of accumulation and disorder. Trying to keep them tidy and to separate various objects of the same type in different spaces will certainly help you find them again. And it will save you from having to mess up the room every time you can't find something. If possible, it is always recommended to use drawers with dividers, a bit like the cutlery drawer.

8. Sort vertically. In this case, or we do not mean like towers of Babel, or rather the boxes which contains various objects. To avoid this situation, it may be useful to use shelf extensions, in order to also increase the capacity of furniture, cabinets and cupboards.

9. Store heavy items at the bottom. This is a basic rule to avoid unnecessary risks on stairs and ladders in an attempt to lift or retrieve heavy objects from shelves or boxes located very high. Therefore, keep the heaviest objects on the ground or, even better, at waist height, it will be easier to lift them to move them.

www.ingramcontent.com/pod-product-compliance
Lightning Source LLC
Chambersburg PA
CBHW071155120626
46546CB00006B/2273